How to Be
The World's Best Fisherman

HOW TO BE
THE WORLD'S BEST FISHERMAN

Bob Nudd

with Keith Elliott

BOXTREE

First published in Great Britain in 1993
by Boxtree Limited

10 8 6 4 2 1 3 5 7 9

Edited by Helen Douglas Cooper
Designed by Millons Design
Typeset by SX Composing, Rayleigh, Essex
Printed and bound in Great Britain by Butler and
Tanner Ltd, Frome for

Boxtree Limited
Broadwall House
21 Broadwall
London SE1 9PL

A CIP catalogue entry for this book
is available from the British Library.

ISBN 1 85283 419 6

CONTENTS

ACKNOWLEDGEMENTS

*T*his is not a normal fishing book. It's not a how to catch-'em, though I hope there is plenty in here that will give even good anglers new ideas. Nor is it a personal ego trip, telling you my life story, though there's some of that here too. I've tried to combine both elements to produce a readable book that will entertain as well as inform. To do this, I've sometimes had to hop to and fro, and break away from a neat, chronological sequence. My apologies if this sometimes gets a little confusing.

I'd like to thank my wife Bernadette for putting up with my passion for angling, and for not just allowing me to fish but actually encouraging it. Her influence and support has been a huge factor in my success during the past two years.

I would also like to thank Terry Freeman, boss of Browning, who has been so immensely supportive in helping me to achieve what I have done, and to Pete Clapperton, without whose drive, determination and friendship I would probably still be doing a very dull job. My thanks as well to my three daughters for putting up with a father who wasn't there as much as he should have been. This book is very much for you, for being so understanding about it.

My thanks also to Keith Elliott, angling correspondent of *The Independent*, who has played such a big part in putting this book together, and to the many, many people all over the world who have helped me in my fishing. And finally, a special thanks to all those who lent me pictures, including *Angling Times*, Rodney Coldron, Martin Founds, Nick Chaffer of Challenge Advertising and Anglers' World Holidays.

Bob Nudd
1993

Never throw your fish back. Put them back carefully so that you can continue to have good fishing.

FOREWORD

I first met Bob Nudd in Ireland in the early 1980s. Although he had not been fishing for very long, it was obvious to me that he had the potential to be a very good angler. He was mixing with the right kind of anglers and was living and breathing fishing. (He still does.)

He has been a member of the England team since 1984, and picking him was one of the best decisions I ever made. He has developed tremendously, and I believe he is probably the best pole angler in the world. There may be a few others who can do certain things as well as him, but for all-round ability, from fishing 1 m out to 17 or 18 m, there is nobody to touch him.

He plays a vital part in the team preparation because he is so dedicated. He is the perfect team member, and though he has been in the squad for nearly 10 years, he is still willing to listen and learn. He is very open-minded in team talks. And though he may have a reputation as a quiet man, he is often very forthright!

Bob has the ideal temperament. He has been world champion twice, and it can be very hard to stay the same when you achieve the things he has done. But he hasn't let it affect him at all. He doesn't know how to be big-headed.

I am full of admiration for Bob and what he has achieved. For someone who wants to be a top match angler, there could be no better example than Bob Nudd.

Dick Clegg
England team manager

Fishing a bit heavier than normal . . . one of my occasional sea fishing trips.

I

EARLY DAYS

*I*think I was born to be a fisherman, but never realized it until quite late in my life. Most top anglers have had the guidance of a fishing father, uncle or grandfather, but my father, who was a butcher, never saw anything in the sport. Yet almost the first fish I caught were a 3 lb (1.35 kg) roach and a 38 lb (17.25 kg) stingray. Since then I've won the World Championships twice, been in the England team since 1984, collected four team winners' medals, picked up almost every honour in fishing – but I've never caught a roach or a stingray anything like as big as those first ones.

Swinging in another roach, and on my way to the World Championships individual title again.

HOW TO BE THE WORLD'S BEST FISHERMAN

I was born on September 24, 1944 in Caister, just outside Great Yarmouth. When I was four, we moved down to Waltham Abbey in Essex. I've lived in Essex ever since. My earliest memory of fishing is at the age of five, when we lived for a year on a farm at Little Waltham. My older sisters, Jacqueline and Christobel, would take me and my younger sister, Bridget, to a private local lake. Using a cork or a bit of wood as a float, we fished for little roach with bread-paste. I can still shut my eyes and bring back the distinctive aroma that those small roach left on our hands, and the smell of that bread-paste. I think my sisters took me along because they had to keep an eye on me. Funny, but I never really got into fishing then. It was one of the things you did as a youngster, and I was just as interested in other things. It's a bit different now!

When I was about 10, Dad bought our first car, an Austin 7. We used to drive to Yarmouth to see my grandparents. The journey would take five or six hours at 25 mph and the car kept breaking down. Petrol cost 1s 11d a gallon. Sometimes I stayed there all summer. I fished from the pier, but never caught very much.

We were quite a poor family, so every weekend I worked on Wheeler's Farm to earn money. In the summer I would go fruit-picking in the evenings, too. When the farmer, Claude Seymour, got to know me, he would let me do everything. I was driving tractors from the age of 12, even though I could hardly reach the clutch. Most of all, I loved working the mechanical muck-spreader, which spread manure everywhere. I think its appeal was the mess it made! I even milked the cows – it was all done manually then. I remember playing with my best friend, David Newman, and squirting the milk into each other's mouths. I would often be there at dawn and leave after dark. For that, I earned perhaps 2 shillings for working all day Saturday. It seemed a lot of money in those days.

Schooldays at Broomfield Secondary Modern were a happy time. I was hopeless at English but I loved maths. It was to prove very useful later in my life. When I was 13, I joined the army cadets. There wasn't as much evening television in those days and no computers. Youngsters created their own entertainment and went out a lot more. I was very good at shooting, but when you're 14 years old the recoil from those .303 rifles really whacks you. I was quite good at boxing, too, and once knocked out my sergeant! I rose to the rank of sergeant myself before I left. I was good at most sports and played cricket for the school, but I never really had time for much outside activity. I always seemed to be working to earn money.

Anyway, the cadets gave me my second taste of fishing. The captain, whose name I've forgotten, was very keen on piking, so a couple of us would travel to Boreham Lakes with him. It was pretty barbaric: we impaled a poor live roach on huge trebles and chucked it out. We caught a few pike, not very big, but one day my livebait was taken by a massive roach of 3 lb. It was weighed on proper scales, and I got my picture on the front page of *Angling Times*. I've never had a roach anywhere near as big since. It's strange how we use such delicate tackle to tempt roach now, and there I was catching this giant fish on a wire trace and snap tackle.

I stayed on an extra year at school, and left just before I was 17. I wanted to go into the Royal Engineers. I passed all the exams and even got the travel passes and rail warrants to turn up at Aldershot barracks; then for some reason I decided not to go. I still don't really know why. My father was insistent that I should not follow him into the butchery trade. But it was a good time to be young, because there were lots of jobs around. You could pretty well decide where you wanted to go. I didn't really know. I was not quite 17 and the only things I was really interested in were going out at night and chasing girls. The job didn't really matter.

I joined the largest local employer, Marconi, as a sheet-metal worker on £2.50 a week. To boost my money, I worked Saturdays and sometimes Sundays. I was good with my hands and only a year later I ended up, at 18, on piecework. This made a huge difference and I was soon earning about £20 a week, which was a lot of money in the early 1960s. I was still living at home. I never even thought about fishing. My interests were girls and work.

At 21, my life seemed mapped out in front of me. I had married Susan, a girl who worked at Marconi, and I had just got a staff job as an instructor in the training centre. It seemed to offer very good job prospects and I only had to work Saturday mornings, so it had the advantage of giving me a little more flexibility.

Marconi had a very enthusiastic fishing club, but I didn't get involved in it until I was 23. I can't even remember exactly how I started. Everyone else I talk to can remember their first rod, reel and every bit of equipment, but even talking to some of my friends from those days, I'm no wiser as to exactly how I got into it. Someone must have asked me to go fishing with them, and I went to one of the matches. I can't even remember where my first tackle came from. I suppose someone must have lent me a bit, but it wasn't long before I went out and bought my own.

My first rod was a hollow-glass one called the Sealey Blue Match: state-of-the-art then, but heavy as six of today's carbon rods.

One angler who was a big influence was Dennis Willis, who was then an apprentice under me. I remember him winning the first match he ever fished with Marconi with 10 lb (4.5 kg) of dace, quite a weight in those days. We went on the upper Chelmer together to practise, and he showed me how to fish a stick float and present a waggler properly. Before very long, most of the Marconi matches were won either by Dennis or myself. The year after I came close to breaking the world record in Ireland, Dennis took the record himself, weighing in with 207 lb 8 dr (93.90 kg) of roach. It stood as the record until Pete Burrell – also a member of my Essex County team – had 258 lb (140.25 kg).

Marconi had its own waters: Boreham Pits, part of the River Chelmer and one or two other lakes. Mainly I fished on the Chelmer. In those days we never travelled far for our fishing, even though I had my own car. I just wish that I'd kept records of those early times. Though I was very green, I won a couple of matches right from the start. Even in those days, I tried to work out what was required to catch fish at that particular time and in that particular place. It was my first and earliest lesson, and it's one that still holds good. If you turn up on a water and don't know the methods needed, you might just as well not be there. No matter how good an angler you are, you can be made to look a fool by somebody who knows exactly what to do.

The Marconi matches were either on the River Chelmer or the Marconi lakes, and once I had worked out the methods, I never really practised much. In addition, I was still working on Saturday mornings, so the only real chance of fishing was on Sundays, and on Wednesday evenings in the summer.

In those days the Chelmer was a fine river. In winter the club's matches were held on the upper river, a shallow, fast-running stretch, and during summer on the slower, deeper lower river. I liked the shallower water best because it held dace and I've always enjoyed dace fishing. We used 3.65 m rods, open-face reels and stick float. Bait was mostly double maggot, though bigger baits like flake or cheese would work well because big chub lived there as well as dace. I just seemed to know what to do from the start. On my very first match on the upper Chelmer, I drew one of the renowned chub holes. I freelined a big lump of cheese on my float fishing rod and it went round straight away. I landed a chub of about 2 lb (900 g), which

was an enormous fish to me then. I don't think I won the match, but it was quite a start!

The normal way to fish the upper river was with a stick float running down your peg, because it was shallow and clear, and the fish tended to hang back even if you were loose-feeding maggots. On shallow waters it's often possible to bring the fish right up to you and catch them faster. However, this can be a disadvantage because you are far more likely to spook them, whereas if you keep them at a distance, you can often catch all day. We fished quite crude – size 16 hooks and double maggot – although it was right for dace. I still don't use a small hook for dace fishing because they wriggle so much that they often get away on a 22 or 24. Dace have big mouths relative to their size and they're very fast eaters. They don't inspect the bait as carefully as a roach.

Almost every match is pegged-down nowadays, but then we often fished rovers, where we could pick our peg and even move if it wasn't fishing well. We would walk along the river, fancy the look of a swim and just drop in there. And sometimes we would be 50 or 60 yards from the nearest angler. A weight of 6 lb (2.70 kg) was usually enough to win. We weren't very skilful at catching fish then. With the skill I have today those pegs would be worth up to 15 lb (6.8 kg), but it was still good fishing, and the upper Chelmer was my favourite of all the Marconi waters.

Soon after I started fishing, a massive cyanide pollution wiped out all the fish in the lower Chelmer. But I fished a few matches there before that happened. It held roach, perch and dace, and it was very good. It's recovered a little now, but today you would only get about 50 anglers at a match. Then, the Chelmer Championships would attract about 500. It was *the* local fishing event of the year. There was a big marquee and coaches to take people to their pegs.

After the pollution had wiped the fish out, the Chelmer was restocked, and some lunatic decided that the giant bream in Abberton reservoir were just the thing for the river. It was shallow, even in the lower stretches, so half the time they were swimming with their backs out of the water. I caught one in a match and weighed in 9 lb (4.10 kg), and that wasn't one of the big ones! I still didn't win the match, though. Somebody had two for 16 lb (7.25 kg).

My other early match venue was Boreham Pits at Chelmsford, which still fish well. We fished there most of the summer, switching to the rivers about October when the lakes started to go off. One lake had lots of tiny roach, about 30 to the pound. They must have been stunted because there were hardly any better fish. I worked out the way to catch the roach, and fished on the drop for them, which at the time was a pretty revolutionary method. I had a wonderful run in evening matches and won almost all of them, using a short pole. Nowadays, I would use a specialist pole called a whip, which demands a particular style of fishing.

FISHING THE WHIP

Whips are for surface fishing or shallow water where you are looking to take lots of fish quickly, lifting most of them straight out. There's no elastic to worry about. You cast overhead and strike with your wrist. Casting should be done from the wrist rather than with the arm. The action is a flick rather than a cast. Whip is a good name, because it defines that casting action. Whips are designed for casting very small floats overhead without breaking or damaging the pole. The long poles of today are designed for a different purpose, which I'll talk about later.

The great thing about whips is that they are cheap. A good 4-metre carbon whip will only cost about £50, though you can pay much more for the best high-modulus carbon. They are all telescopic, which gives you a slimmer pole and, more importantly, the flexible action needed for this type of fishing. It's true that you can adapt your normal pole for close-in fishing, but the whip has a lot more give than an ordinary pole, and because you are usually fishing on a flick tip, rather than with elastic, this 'give' is very important. The average 4-metre whip should be fairly stiff in the middle with a very fine flick tip. That fine tip gives the right casting action, like a little catapult, for propelling out very small floats. Because of this flexibility, it's surprising what can be landed on a whip. You can get carp, tench, and as I write this, I have just read about a 5 lb 8 oz (2.5 kg) pike landed on a whip.

For general use, I think someone just starting to use whips should buy a 4- or 5-metre one. You can always take one joint off by pulling the whole thing back through itself to give you a shorter pole. For gudgeon, you might use only 1.5 m. The maximum length for single-handed casting with most whips is about 5 metres, but with the very expensive ones you can cast light floats at 6 and even 7 metres.

Catching on the whip at Holme Pierrepont.

FLICK-TIP CONNECTION

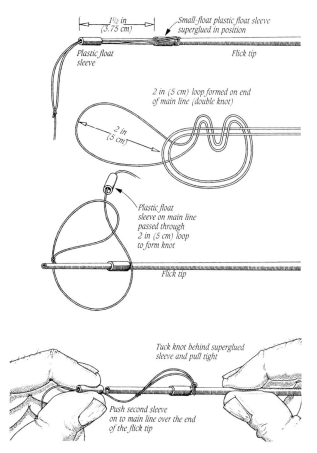

_1½ in (3.75 cm)_

Small-float plastic float sleeve superglued in position

Plastic float sleeve

Flick tip

2 in (5 cm) loop formed on end of main line (double knot)

_2 in (5 cm)_

Plastic float sleeve on main line passed through 2 in (5 cm) loop to form knot

Flick tip

Tuck knot behind superglued sleeve and pull tight

Push second sleeve on to main line over the end of the flick tip

I never bother about changing the tips of whips, except for gudgeon fishing, because usually they are quite fine enough. I adapt the end by using a connection I learnt in Italy about eight years ago. I superglue a piece of stiff sleeving on to the tip, about 1 in (2.5 cm) from the top, then put a loop in my main line, and loop this over the sleeving. I then pull another stiff sleeve, already on the main line, over it. I find the sleeving prevents tangles and doesn't add any weight.

If I'm catching lots of little fish close in, I always fish with a barbless hook, except when I'm fishing for bleak. I try to get away with as big a hook as possible because roach and bleak in particular are going to be taken on the drop, and will be quite active. The strike is important too. A sideways strike is needed, often quite hard, and it should be made in the direction that will bring the fish straight to your unhooking hand.

Bleak on the whip

Bleak are the only fish for which I use a barb and this is a tip I picked up from the Italians. It helps to stop the maggot being blown off. But don't strike with bleak, just lift into them so they are hooked in the soft skin inside the mouth. A smooth action is the secret. If you jerk, fish will fall off all over the place. The whip's soft tip cushions your strike and doesn't put too much strain on a lightly-hooked fish. When bleak are hooked right, you can just pull the hook straight out of that soft skin. There's no need to fiddle around shaking them or waggling the hook. The only time this doesn't work is if the hook is in the bottom lip. Most Italians unhook every fish. They don't flick them off or put them over the wrist, as I've seen some anglers doing. It's all down to a smooth action, and it certainly doesn't slow the Italians down.

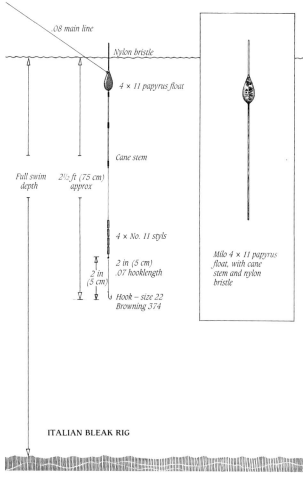

.08 main line

Nylon bristle

4 × 11 papyrus float

Cane stem

Full swim depth

2½ ft (75 cm) approx

4 × No. 11 styls

2 in (5 cm) .07 hooklength

_2 in (5 cm)_

Hook – size 22 Browning 374

Milo 4 × 11 papyrus float, with cane stem and nylon bristle

ITALIAN BLEAK RIG

I have caught bleak at a rate of nine a minute, which works out at 540 in an hour. Some Italians can do 1,000 in an hour with everything going right, and I'm told that all members of the Italian World Championship team are capable of catching at a rate of 500 an hour.

However, getting the fish in is only half the story. There are other key factors, like feeding and presenting the bait to the fish in the fastest way. I know that a lot of anglers watch the maggot. I used to do that before I learnt the Italian method, which involves watching the float. That said, I know that some very big weights of bleak have been taken on the River Wye by watching the maggot. Others, like the old River Lea bleak-anglers Ade Scutt and Bob Massey, used a thicker line and ran their nail along it near the hook so it curled up. Bob Massey had a famous phrase to describe bleak coming really fast: 'You know you're catching quick when you've got one coming in on the hook and two down the funnel [meaning still going down the net]'. But overall, I think the Italian method which I use is the best.

The Italians work on the principle that bleak are attracted by noise, and use a very short hook length – 2 in (5 cm) or even shorter. All the weight, perhaps four No 11 or No 12 styl leads, is against the hook knot. The Italians always use styls for their bleak fishing because they make more noise than shot. When you cast, the noise of those weights hitting the water attracts the bleak. They come up in the water to find out what's happening. That's when you get the bite. I've seen an Italian angler cast three times, hitting the water, then letting it go. He wasn't feeding at all. This method also seems to bring bigger bleak.

You rarely need to fish light for bleak. They are so aggressive in their feeding that you can fish fairly heavy. And when you're catching a lot of fish, it's easy to break on very light lines. I use 0.07, or even 0.09 if I can get away with it. Hooks would be size 20 or 22. The Italians like a long-shank hook. They thread on the maggot or pinkie so that the whole of it is on the shank, and use an oldish maggot. The Italians breed tough-skinned maggots by rolling them in damp, extra-hard paper, not quite cardboard, and putting them in a fridge for about a month. The maggots don't turn into casters, but remain in a state of suspended animation and get a really tough skin. The older a maggot gets, the harder it becomes. The Italians prefer pinkies for bleak fishing, and can catch up to 50 fish on one of these tough-skinned specials.

Depth is a key factor in bleak fishing. The method I've been talking about works best in shallow water of 2-3 ft,

and when bleak are feeding right up in the water. There are times when you have to go deep to catch them. The important point about them is that even in midwinter, bleak have to feed because they have to move. Bleak will feed no matter how cold it is. I won three midwinter Lea matches on the trot with bleak weights of 11 lb (5 kg), 12 lb (5.45 kg) and 14 lb (6.35 kg).

I generally start at 3 ft (1 m), but the vital thing is to find the depth at which the fish are feeding, and rather than drop through to that depth, get the bait to the fish as quickly as possible. Bear in mind that bleak nearly always take on the drop. They do not want a stationary bait. Don't leave your bait in too long; pull it out and recast. Bleak fishing is hard work! Even with all that weight, bleak will often grab a bait as soon as it hits the water. The Italian rig allows you to see this immediately. Always strike at once because bleak always get hold of a bait; they never just inspect it.

Feeding is another key factor in keeping bleak in your peg and responsive to the bait. I use Van den Eynde Surface Cloud, which is a very light mix that hovers in the water. It hasn't got any food value so it doesn't fill up the fish. The Italians feed a similar mix that is very sloppy and wet, and theirs has a high content of silkworm cocoons. This seems to put the fish into a feeding frenzy.

I put a few fluorescent pinkies in the cloud if joker is barred. If joker is allowed, I feed just a few joker but fish a fluorescent pinkie, which is a brilliant bleak bait, on the hook. The bleak will come straight into the cloud, but the Italians tend to fish just a little bit short or just beyond it. I don't yet know why. They do a lot more of it than we do, but I just fish in or around the cloud.

On running water, you should fish pretty much the same way except when it's running hard and you're fishing for bigger bleak. Then loose-fed maggot is all the feed you need. On canals and rivers, roach and dace will often be feeding underneath on the jokers that drop through. It's worth setting up a second rig and spending at least a few minutes seeing if there are bonus fish around, especially in the last hour.

When feeding for bleak, remember that you cast and feed, but that you will be catching off the feed you put in on the previous cast. If you get a hook caught in your jumper or keepnet, remember to keep feeding, or the fish will go. You're aiming to create a constant cloud of feed. Once that cloud has dispersed, the bleak will be on the move looking for something else. They don't hover and wait, like roach will.

Bleak move around a lot. The obvious thing to do is to alter your depth, or fish further down your peg. You might fish several places in your peg, but keep feeding in the same place. Most times when bleak fishing, you will have a really good spell and then it will ease off. It goes on like this through the match. You sometimes have to fish further out for them in the later stages of a match, so if you've been catching at 3.5 m, you might find that later on you have to go to 5 m.

When I came back from my first trip to Italy, I brought back pith floats with a cane stem and nylon bristle. You don't want a metal stem for bleaking. You want to cast the weight, not the float. The shot shouldn't be fighting against the float. When fishing to hand, you should use a light-bodied float. I always fish top and bottom, but I know that northern anglers prefer to fish bottom-only. It's a personal matter, perhaps, but I think top and bottom gives better presentation, particularly with bleak.

Occasionally I use bottom-only when I've been bread-punch fishing on canals, where I've wanted to keep the pole away from my float area because the water's clear and I'm not getting that many bites. If you fish top and bottom and it's a bit windy, you will find the float skids around too much.

Whip fishing with this simple rig is a very good way for you to discover your weaknesses. It teaches you how to hold a pole, how to handle a fish quickly without letting go of the pole and how to feed. The ability to feed with your left hand if you're right-handed, and vice versa, is critical for speed fishing. When you are catching a lot of fish, you don't want to keep switching hands. With soft groundbait, you can use an underarm scoop, but with wet feed you have to learn to flick it with your fingers, just as you would flick maggots underarm. So speed fishing with a whip is all about rhythm. It's a lovely method because very little can go wrong. You just flick overhead, the tackle falls in a straight line because of the catapult effect from the whip, and you rarely get any tangles.

I have been talking about bleak all this time, but fishing for small roach is very similar, though you would usually space out the droppers. Roach, even small ones, are a little more cautious than bleak. They take more carefully and want to see a more naturally falling bait. They are not quite as active as bleak, so the bait wants to fall through the water naturally, from top to bottom. Occasionally you will catch with the weight bunched, and that's obviously the quickest way to catch, but as it gets harder you will probably have to space them.

Gudgeon on the whip

So far I've just talked about surface-feeding fish, but in the past couple of years, the whip has really showed its potential by taking some very large gudgeon catches. When I know I'm on for a net of gudgeon, I use a cut-back tip so it is quite stiff. Most whips have very fine tips, and sometimes if you are catching quantities of large gudgeon, they actually pull when you strike, which wastes a lot of time. With the cut-back tip, you can pull even big gudgeon straight out of the water. It doesn't get the chance to fight; it's straight into your hand. This method works best with fairly large hooks, 20 or 21s. If gudgeon are more difficult to catch and you have to use small floats, then you have to resort to the finer tips.

The best hook for gudgeon is a barbless long-shank. I use an SA10 by Katsuchi, which is a high-carbon hook. Gudgeon have a meaty mouth like a barbel or chub and they don't come off the hook very easily. Even a micro-barb is too much. I sometimes open the hook up slightly so it's just pointing out a little bit, which hooks the fish a lot easier. There is no way you are going to straighten the hook on a gudgeon!

Always try to fish as large as you can. On bloodworm you can usually get away with a 22, though hook patterns and sizes vary tremendously. When I'm bloodworm fishing for a lot of gudgeon, I just hook the worm through the middle, which prevents too much of the worm hanging down on one side. Whenever fish are difficult to catch on bloodworm or you are missing bites, just hook the blood-worm straight through the middle instead of near the top end. It can make quite a difference.

Gudgeon are bottom-feeders, so you want to get everything down to them as quickly as possible. This means using a short hooklength, something like 2 in (5 cm) which brings all the shot and olivette very close to the hooklength. My nearest shot would probably be right where I've tied the hooklength, with the olivette only 2 in (5 cm) above that. And if they are feeding ravenously, I might even pull the olivette down on the dropper so everything is immediate. I always want to see the bite as soon as it happens.

If I am fishing bloodworm, I nearly always use ground-bait for gudgeon. The ideal is a little damp leam mixed with joker, with groundbait added to make plum-sized balls that are fairly solid and more than 50 per cent joker. Depending on how many fish I am expecting, I would feed four of these. Gudgeon will often be in the fairly shallow water on the far or near-bank shelf. If it's cold, they may

*Mixing my groundbait
before the 1992 world
match in Northern Ireland.
I needed heavy feed to
combat the flow.*

move into slightly deeper water. Usually the fish are going to be on your shelf when you start, as long as you don't cause too much disturbance. That's why it's best to set up well back from the bank on canals. If there are a lot of fish about, the near bank is the quickest way to catch them. However, quite often, particularly near the end of matches, you may have to switch to the far bank.

Always use a plummet to find the point where the shelf slopes away from you. If it is sloping hard, you have to be very careful that your feed doesn't roll away from where you are fishing. If you are fishing on the bottom of a shelf, you can throw your feed straight at the float and know it is going to stay still. Four balls is only an average. If I think it will be hard, I would only put one ball in; if I think it is going to be really good, I might feed six.

If fish are coming fast, I will keep adding a small ball of feed when I'm using joker. I am a little more wary if bloodworm is banned, because other baits can fill the fish. There is no simple answer about when or even how to feed. I won a match on the Trent and Mersey Canal with 9 lb (4.10 kg) of gudgeon the first time I fished it. I was flicking in little bits of very sloppy groundbait with a few joker. Imagine the scene underwater: there was this rich cloud from the groundbait and 10 or 12 jokers filtering down. I was catching gudgeon up in the water, using a light rig with my shots spaced down the line.

On other days, you have to get everything down hard. If you can feed joker so that it filters through the water, it is the best way to spark roach into feeding, although you can't always do it when you're fishing at 12 m or more. It would be lovely if you could flick a tiny bit of groundbait or leam on your float every time, but very few people can consistently feed that accurately. On canals you can usually feed two or three lines, but you need to swap around to get the best from the peg. If you've got gudgeon on the whip line all day, then you'll probably win the match.

If bloodworm is banned and maggot is the key bait, the secret is not to feed too heavily and fill the fish up. But I would still use a little groundbait. Fluorescent pinkie is a good bait for gudgeon, perhaps because it looks a bit like bloodworm. Quite often, feeding joker and fishing a fluorescent pinkie will sort out a bigger stamp of gudgeon. So if you are getting pestered with little fish on bloodworm, put a pinkie on. You probably won't catch as fast, but you can sometimes pick up a bigger stamp of fish. I hardly ever bother with using more than one bloodworm for gudgeon as it's a waste of time. Choose a big bloodworm and hook it through the middle.

Other species on the whip

The other main use of the whip is for roach and perch, particularly in the summer on lakes when the fish are fairly active. The whip is ideal for caster fishing close in because you have perfect control, with a little float and the bait dropping through naturally. You can't achieve this with rod and line because it's far too heavy. I've had plenty of double-figure weights in evening matches using this method. One of my favourite waters is Lake Meadows at Billericay, where the best weight I've had is 13 lb 8 oz (6.10 kg) in three hours. This comprised a lot of small fish to start with on pinkie and groundbait while feeding caster 1 metre further out, and in the last 45 minutes switching to a slightly longer whip and caster for quality roach.

I like to fish a whip standing up, except on canals, because it gets you another metre out. My rig would generally be four No. 10s and a 0.07 main line. The main line should be as fine as possible, because when you are fishing a whip, you have a fair bit of line from tip to float. Control is dependent on the wind and the wind pressure against the line, so line diameter is absolutely crucial for casting and for presentation once you are out there. It shouldn't be long before you get a bite, but that float can soon skid round. The difference between a 0.09 main line and a 0.06 is incredible. It is so much easier to cast and mend. It should always be a high-tech line, but because of the elasticity of the pole tip, a pre-stretched line is still all right.

My favourite float for this style of fishing is pith with a cane stem and nylon bristle. This float is ultra light and follows the weight that you are casting. Carbon stems are all right but cane is ideal, with a pith or papyrus body. It should be an inverted pear shape, slim at the top so you can see on-the-drop bites. This shape of float clears the water easily. Shot it right down to the tip of the bristle.

Again, the strike should always be sideways. If you strike upwards and you've got a big fish on, it comes straight out of the water and will usually go straight back in and break you. I normally strike quite hard to the left. The strike pulls a fish away from the shoal. As you strike, you feel the size of it and know immediately whether it is just a straight lift into your hand, or whether you have to net it.

For roach, it is important to realize that a bite can come from the moment the float hits the water to down on the bottom. In summer, roach are usually up in the water. You might be fishing 2 ft (60 cm) or more off bottom, and you have to adjust the shot or styls (the latter give a slower drop, but I think it makes very little difference), changing their spacing to see the bites. The more aggressive the bites, the tighter you can put your shots and the quicker you can see what's happening. Sometimes I pull all the shot together within 2 in (5 cm) of the hook. With bleak, your bait would be 'dead' once it had reached the depth at which you had set the float. But this doesn't apply quite so much for roach, because the groundbait is creating a cloud into which the fish are coming. Lifting your float a little and just moving it slightly can induce a bite.

I will often go through a lot of groundbait. If it is clearly encouraging fish to feed, use a dry mix and put in a fair-sized ball every cast. This mix (I use Van den Eynde Surface Cloud), which doesn't have any real feed value in it and is just to create a cloud) breaks up as soon as it hits the water. For summer roach fishing, I might add pinkies to it, but not joker because it attracts too small fish. With groundbait that hardly binds together, you need a special throwing technique. You have to pick it up and throw underarm, all in one movement. As you pick it up and scoop it, you let your hand release it. Although it's almost disintegrating in the air, it still falls in one spot. You can't throw a dry mix in any other way. You are limited to distance – about 6 metres is the limit.

Pinkie as hookbait has the advantage that you can catch more fish on the same bait than bloodworm. In the summer, you should be aiming to catch a fish every 30 seconds and it's not necessary to keep checking your bait. You soon get an idea of how many bites you are getting or whether you have to replace the bait. Often you can catch four or five fish on the same maggot. And I always use barbless hooks.

Feeding casters on a slightly longer line will often attract big fish. I've often caught 2 lb (900 g) bream on a whip. The bream are as surprised as you are! You strike, feel the weight and the next second they are at the top and you've netted them. Sometimes you will hook a tench or a carp, but on 4 m and 0.07 line, you don't have a lot of leeway. They will often break you, but if this starts to happen regularly, it's time to switch to elastic. However, it won't be as efficient at catching the smaller fish because you can't get that neat flick with the stiffer tip. If you hook a little fish, the elastic comes out and it bounces all over the place. But it may be worth the switch if it will bring you a bonus 2 lb (900 g) tench.

Near the end of a match, it's worth trying hard on the bottom because there are often a few bigger fish grubbing round or hanging back. You don't always have to cast into your feed; you can sometimes cast a little away from it and get those bigger fish.

It must be the old days; you would never find me sitting on a wicker tackle-box now.

I know a lot of people use a whip for chopped-worm fishing, but I prefer a normal pole and short line. There are a number of reasons for this. First, there is the possibility of catching big fish. A perch of 1 lb (450 g) or larger will put up quite a scrap and the last thing you want is to lose a bonus fish like that. Chopped worm also needs to be moved quite frequently, and you need to be over the top of your float. You can't move it with a whip as well as you need to. You need to pick the worm up, drop it, pull it one way, pull it the other.

Whip fishing should be seen as the best method for catching gudgeon, or small fish that are feeding really aggressively on the drop. However, if you're sitting for 10 minutes waiting for a bite, you shouldn't be on the whip.

EARLY MATCHES

However, I never knew any of that in those early days. I just used a little pole and fished a maggot on the drop. And though I loved fishing the small roach lake, my favourite was the middle lake, which held some lovely crucian carp,

The end of a busy day; a net of small roach from Ten Mile Bank.

tench, proper carp and skimmer bream. The third lake held skimmers and bigger bream. Some were big fish, but you couldn't rely on them.

In those days you drew a lake, and picked your peg on that lake. I always hoped I would draw the crucian lake. I worked out a method to catch them, fishing close in with a small float and a very soft flour-and-water paste. I felt confident of winning if I drew there because they were good-sized fish, 12 oz (340 g) to 1 lb (450 g), and my method seemed to work for them all the time. A catch of 8-10 lb

was usually needed to win. I love catching crucians anyway because they are so beautiful. The main problem with crucians is hooking those finicky bites because they have very soft mouths and come off easily. This is less of a problem now, thanks to poles with soft elastic.

There were few poles then, except some early hollow-glass Lercs that went up to 7 metres and were really only useful at shorter distances for small fish. It was mainly float-fishing with a running line, though you would probably use a swingtip on the bream lake. I didn't really enjoy drawing this lake because it meant waiting for fish. People say to me, 'Oh, you must have loads of patience being an angler,' but I'm the most impatient person in the world. If something's not happening. I'm not interested. I have to make something happen.

I love catching fish and their size doesn't matter. If I win the match, that's a bonus. It's good to win, but it's not so important. If you're obsessed with winning, you are losing sight of what fishing is all about. Go and play darts or table tennis instead. Kevin Ashurst is the same. We often pleasure-fish together on the Bann in Northern Ireland, where you can catch 100 lb (45 kg) of big roach in a day. People ask whether I get bored just catching the same sort and size of fish, but the pleasure of it is always there.

Club matches in those days also meant coach trips to other places, mostly the Fens and East Anglia. We went to the Norfolk Broads, where there were a lot of bream, and Bungay Common on the Waveney. I can remember winning a club outing with 12 lb (5.45 kg) of chub that I caught on the stick float from under a big overhanging tree. Those coach trips weren't really serious matches, more a social event with 30 people going for a coach ride with a bit of fishing thrown in. The great thing about Marconi was that I never experienced any jealousy over my immediate success. It was a very friendly club.

When I started at Marconi, I went out on a few boat-fishing trips before I ever started match fishing. On my very first boat trip, I caught a 38 lb (17.25 kg) stingray out

One of my treasured cuttings from Angling Times *at the start of my match fishing career.*

Smash and grab raid

Norwich Open

ESSEX match anglers carried out another daylight robbery in Norwich — this time grabbing the money from the top four placings in the Norwich Motor Company Open, on the River Wensum.

Drawing the Coal Yard reach, Bob Nudd led an Essex National quartet with 11 lb 13 oz, followed by Andy Cornwall with 9 lb 11½ oz, Gordon Blanks with 9 lb 9½ oz and Barry Charlick, with 7 lb 11½ oz.

It was pole fishing "par excellence", that none of the other competitors could live with, and boosted Bob Nudd's total winnings this season to £1,800. All the fish were small roach taken on single bronze maggot.

Result: 1 R. Rudd, Essex, 11 lb 13 oz; 2 A. Cornwall, Essex, 9 lb 11½ oz; 3 G. Blanks, Essex, 9 lb 9½ oz; 4 C. Charlick, Essex, 7 lb 11½ oz; 5 T. Sturman, Norwich, 6 lb 10 oz.

● RIGHT: Bob Nudd

The Essex Cats and the winter league trophy. The one with the filmstar looks holding the trophy is me! The mad professor in the back row is Pete Clapperton. He was a one-off even then.

from Bradwell. I've never landed a sea fish as big since. I caught it on a cane rod and I was about to grab hold of the fish when the skipper knocked me out of the way and chopped off its tail, which of course carries the sting. Nowadays, it would be put back in the sea.

The quality of my own fishing improved so much at Marconi in a couple of years that I was fishing for them in the Essex Winter League, one of the biggest in the country with 15 teams. Matches were mostly on the River Stour at Sudbury. We were just a team of club anglers, but in 1970 we won the league and got to the semi-finals. It was on the Bristol Avon, and I was hopelessly out of my depth. I never went down to practise as I would now; I just turned up on the day. The Avon is a big, deep, flowing river and I had no idea how to handle it. My swim was a corker. A big log was sticking out of the water and it really looked the part. I caught about 3 lb (1.35 kg) of dace and the peg must have been worth at least 10 lb (4.5 kg). As a team, we came eighth out of eight. The match was won by Birmingham, who were miles ahead of us in ability.

I was now 26 and virtually on the open match circuit. I had more spare time because I was only working three Saturdays out of four, but I already had three daughters – Sharon, Debra and Tracey. When I look back, it's astonishing to realize that I had progressed to this stage in just three years without doing any of the classic things such as learning everything from a father or friend, or even spending time watching successful anglers. While people in Marconi had helped me with various things, I had worked most of it out by myself in the little time I had available – Sundays and the occasional evening trip.

Circumstances forced me to approach it in this way, but it's not the best way to become a good match angler. Learning from other people is much quicker and you must never be frightened to ask. Even now, I would never be afraid, or think I was too important, to go up to another angler and ask his advice on fishing a particular water. Local knowledge is the best way to learn.

Some keen anglers find it impossible to make the jump from club matches to opens because of domestic problems, time considerations and so on, but generally there's a natural progression once you start winning club matches regularly. You want to try out your skills against a higher class of competition, to drive yourself on. Those early opens, however, can be a culture shock. They certainly were for me. I wasn't winning anything. I was doing all right in my section, but suddenly there were a lot of anglers who were as good as me and better. Even though the

standard is far higher now, and winning in those days was a lot easier, I had become pools fodder.

Weighing-in during a match run by Marconi, I met the winner, Barry Charlick, and his friend Peter Clapperton, who has been a huge influence on my life. Both were really sea anglers, but they had decided to have a go at match fishing (in fact it was their first match, and Barry won it!) We got on well and I asked them to join the Marconi team. They refused, but fell in love with match fishing so we got to know each other well. Like me, they wanted to do better. So we formed a team called the Three Cups, with Peter as captain. Several other good local matchmen joined us. Being able to share my knowledge and learn from others made a great difference. It's a good lesson for any angler who wants to improve. Get in with a team of quality anglers, and you will learn from them. The final chapter talks a lot about team fishing.

We did well as a team, and might have won the winter league, except that in the final match, one of us fished the wrong peg and was disqualified. He would have won the match, which made it even worse. I don't think Peter has forgiven him yet! But straight afterwards we had the opportunity to improve further when we were asked to join the Cats, the top match group in Essex.

Among their best-known anglers was Gerry Allen. Other members of the team included Dave Ward, Dennis Russell, Les Drury and Gordon Blanks. Gordon has been a close friend since those early days. He's a fine angler who's won a lot of top honours, and he even captained the American team in the World Championships at one stage.

By 1966 I was living in Chelmsford, not far from Peter. I had a bronze Corsair that always seemed to go wrong. Whenever I didn't turn up, the others would come round and find me with the bonnet up, hands covered in oil and swearing at the car. Pete, myself, Barry Charlick and Colin Bugg would squash into it with our wicker baskets. We mainly fished the Cam, Stour, Chelmer and Ouse, all local waters. The farthest we went was probably to the North Bank of the Nene to fish for winter leagues.

Bream fishing is a waiting game. I would always prefer to catch 20 lb of roach rather than 20 lb of bream.

1966 was a special year because I won my first open, on the Great Ouse at Offord Cluny. I had learnt that to be successful, you need to find out about a new water, so I had been up there practising. One stretch was slow moving and deep, 12-13 ft (3.65-3.95 m), and in practice I caught roach on caster with a slider – quite an advanced method at the time. But I was an avid reader of all the angling papers, and always keen to try out new things. I had read about slider fishing and made up all my own sliders. At the time, I made all my own floats. Nowadays, the quality is so good that I never bother. I adapt shop-bought ones slightly, but I'll say more about that later (page 121).

At the time, I hadn't learnt that you rarely do as well in a match as in practice. However, in this match I drew the same area and the method worked just as well. The roach fed well all day on caster and the slider, and I won the match with 14 lb (6.35 kg). I didn't have many, but they were all quality fish, between 6 oz (170 g) and 10 oz (285 g). I won £50, which was a lot of money then. And I felt terrific even though, looking back, I was very lucky. There's nothing quite like your first open win, especially as there were a lot of good anglers taking part on Ouse matches back then.

The slider is a much-misunderstood method. I later learnt to fish it properly as a result of my contact with the England team and in particular Ian Heaps. He taught me how to set up a slider and shot it so it doesn't tangle. The two basic points are: don't cast off your bulk shot; and if you don't want tangles, use a fair-sized dropper like a No. 1. The point of any dropper is that you can see what it is doing. You should be able to see when the bulk takes effect, and when the dropper settles. You won't do that with a No.8 on a float taking perhaps three SSG.

In addition, you need to make sure that the distance between hook and dropper is less than the distance between dropper and bulk, and that the distance between bulk shot and stop shot is greater than between bulk and dropper. Work on this principle and you'll never tangle, even if the whole lot goes into the water in a mess. Never cast off your bulk shot – it's a recipe for tangles.

The best way of fishing a slider is to use a loaded float that is heavier than your bulk. When you cast, the bulk shot follows the float. It sometimes goes out looking funny, but as long as you have shotted up properly, it never tangles.

Although you can fish a slider top and bottom, this has now been superseded by the Bolognese method (see pages 142-144), which holds back far better. So generally you would fish bottom only with a stop knot. It's fairly easy to find the depth on a slider, even on flowing water, because of that sizeable dropper. If it doesn't register, you know you're too deep. Use a tiny dropper, and it's much harder to see.

1972 was another memorable year, because I started my own business, in a very small way, with Peter. Our business started with a £20 Commer walkthrough van with a door at the back. We had this idea for a mobile food van because when we turned up at fishing matches, there was never anything to eat or drink. We hand-painted the van bright yellow and wrote on the side, again by hand, Pete and Bob's Mobile Dogs. We did the work during the close season and had the van, nicknamed Big Bertha, all ready for the start of the season. Those were wonderful days, but it was very hard work. I got to know a lot of famous anglers like Ivan Marks through serving them with hot dogs and hamburgers.

Although I was still working at Marconi, the van was bringing in a lot of extra money, especially when we found an evening site in Chelmsford. Soon we were taking money not just at matches, but every night as well. We were earning about £30 a week each out of it.

We got fed up with Big Bertha breaking down and very quickly bought another. We ended up with six converted minivans and Big Bertha, which we couldn't part with. And things were going well, though it was very hard work. There were times when I was only getting two or three hours' sleep a night. When we got back from a match, we had to empty the tackle out and clean the van again ready for the evening. And every angler knows that it's much easier to leave everything in the car, ready for the next day's fishing!

The bread strikes in the early 1970s were one of the turning points of my life. When you've got a hot-dog van and a bread strike comes along, you can't get any rolls and you're out of business. It was lucky that I still had my full-time job at Marconi, where I'd progressed from training apprentices to a time-study engineer in research and development. Then I got on to production engineering. Marconi made a lot of television equipment and we used to run outside broadcast vans, where I worked as production engineer, which was like a troubleshooter. From there I went on to the best job I had there, which was estimating. I did a lot of work on costing underwater naval equipment. It was fascinating and challenging, particularly with inflation running at 20 per cent, but I was coming to realize that you never make a lot of money working for someone else.

The Marconi job gave me security, but the bread strikes made business much more precarious for Peter, so he formed his own company and started making rolls. By now the business had grown so much that I had gone into the wholesale side, buying in hamburgers and hot dogs, and we shared a warehouse. I left Marconi in 1975, when I was 31. I had worked there for 16 years, was progressing well within the company and had a good career there, but it was too limiting. I couldn't fish as much as I wanted, and trying to do two jobs was very hard. I was financially sound with the hot dogs, and the wholesale business.

At first, I worked very hard on the business and it was doing really well. In 1976 I bought my first new car, an Audi 100, and for years I had a new car every year. People were driving my vans in the evenings, and I had Kevin Reid working full-time in the office. As the wholesale business grew, I hired a manager and a couple of office staff, plus two van drivers for deliveries. I ended up with three delivery vans covering all of East Anglia.

Essex Cats soon merged with another match group called The Pack, whose members included Malcolm Felgate and Paul Cornock. They were from the A1 and Harlow area. We became Catpack and had such a strong squad that we dominated the local winter league. In those days I was struggling to get in the team and it took me more than a year to win a regular place. Catpack and other teams such as Roding Valley supplied Essex County for the Nationals, and for other major competitions. Essex County eventually became a match team in its own right, and is now probably the country's top team.

Even in those early days Essex County had some exceptional anglers. There was Tommy Boulton, who's now a tackle dealer in Norwich. There was Jimmy Randall, who fished for England in the World Championships and was undoubtedly one of the country's top matchmen. It also included Micky Thill, who is now America's team captain, and Billy Hughes, who may be the most underrated angler in the country, and who was later to be best man when I re-married.

Mixing with anglers of this quality had a profound effect on me. I was constantly asking questions, watching and learning from them. You can learn a lot from books, but when it comes to knowledge of what's happening on a water on a particular day, what type of fish will feed and so on, there is no substitute for local knowledge. This is why a more mature angler will often be more successful – he's built up this knowledge over 20 or 30 years.

To be good at every technique is very, very difficult. Even within Van den Eynde Essex, where we have some of the country's best anglers, there are some whom you put straight in for one water and leave out on another. Even in our supersquad, there are only two or three who make the team on every venue. But all of the others are learning from them.

Back in the late 1960s, I had been very aware that my expertise was on stillwaters and slow-moving rivers, especially fishing the waggler and a new method called the pole. There were no regular match venues on fast-flowing water in Essex or East Anglia. I would have loved to have been brought up on the Trent. Even now, I only put on a stick float perhaps twice a year.

The Fens were then famous as a bream area. There were tons of them, but I never really got into legering. It stems back to my impatience. I didn't want to sit waiting for that tip to move. Even now, given a choice between fishing on the lead for bream and on the float for roach, I'd prefer the roach – but if I know that I will need to leger to win, I won't hesitate. Too many anglers take their favourite method with them wherever they go. You have to be adaptable to be successful.

In the early and mid 1970s, I was just another keen angler, though as a team we were doing very well. On the north bank of the Nene in one winter league, Catpack won every section. I don't think that's ever been done since. That year Gordon Blanks won his section in every match. I had four section wins and two seconds.

On another occasion I fished an open on some lakes at Fen Drayton, near Cambridge, and finished fourth with 32 lb (14.5 kg) of bream. The bream were all jammed into this bay, so I went back the next day and finished with the biggest weight I had ever taken, more than 200 lb (90 kg) of bream. That was good for me because it was the first time I had ever taken over 100 lb (90 kg). That catch was on the front page of *Angling Times* too!

2

HEADING ABROAD

*I*n the past few years, I've been all over the world, and very soon I'll be spending quite some time bringing our style of fishing to the Americans. However, I was 31 before I even went abroad fishing. In those days, going abroad meant Ireland to an angler, and my very first trip to a country that was to become my second home (and provide me with my second wife, Bernadette) was to the mecca of 1970s Irish competition angling, the River Suck at Ballinasloe – known in the match world simply as Bally. I went there with Gerry Allen and Peter Clapperton, and we were lucky enough to win a team match that attracted Britain's top anglers. Mind you, things didn't start too well. We took several gallons of maggots, but we didn't know how to keep them at the time, so they were roasted by the time we got there. It's so easy to transport maggots when you know how (see page 48).

You don't always have to net big fish. If the bank's right or you're standing in the water, it's quicker to bring a fish to hand.

Big Shannon bream. You can tell these are southern fish because in Northern Ireland the bream rarely top 3 lb.

IRELAND

The trouble with Bally then was that a small clique of people knew it upside-down, and kept everything secret, even the places where there was great pleasure fishing. But we refused to be beaten. We had got a rough idea where to go, and were looking for clues when I spotted some orange peel in the road. Who else but an untidy angler would think of dumping his orange peel straight out of the window? We drove along and saw another bit, and another. We followed a trail of orange peel and got to this channel off the Shannon where the fish came through to spawn. We all had about 150 lb (68 kg) of bream between 4 lb (1.8 kg) and 6 lb (2.7 kg).

We had Ivan Marks to thank for our success in the Bally festival. Gerry, who had been there before, won the match overall, but Peter and I both had good backing weights of big rudd. These rudd lived on the far bank, but they would only be there for a short time. Suddenly they would just come from nowhere and you would catch them for about 20 casts. Then they would go again. But they were big fish, 1 lb (450 g) each, and it didn't take long to build up a weight.

We had seen Ivan catching these beautiful fish in practice, and he was such a wonderful open person that he told me exactly how he did it. It meant throwing a lead with a long tail right against the reeds on the far bank, and fishing with floating maggots. The floating maggots were the secret, and they are so easy to prepare.

You need very fresh bait, preferably still with a good feed spot inside. Old maggots won't float. Riddle the maggots thoroughly to take out all bran, maize and so on. You want pure bait. Put a little water in a bait tub, add a handful of maggots and put the lid on the tub. I use an adapted lid with a square cut in the top. As soon as the maggots get wet they will crawl up the sides, and if there is no lid they will climb straight out. With my system, they hit the top and drop back down.

I have a second bait box with water in it, and every now and again I take a few maggots out of my floaters box and drop them in to check which ones are floating. No matter how well you do it, they don't all float. Even when I have baited a hook with one or two floating maggots and dropped them into the water in front of me to make sure they are floating enough to support the hook, some sink and I have to rebait.

Even though you may think your bait is floating, it may not be, especially when there is a strong tow on the water. You may think you're fishing floaters, but your bait is actually near the bottom. That said, you can sometimes catch fish on a slow-sinking bait by putting on a floater and a sinker, or a floater and an almost-floater. The weight of the hook will make such a bait sink slowly, and it can be very attractive to fish.

Looking back, that Bally win was an amazing result. Perhaps it was my lucky hat, which in those days wasn't the white cap that has become my trademark but a German paratrooper-style hat that was good for keeping the ears warm in the winter! We tried again for the following two years to win the Bally, but never did any good. Those lovely rudd disappeared, and with the bream fishing being so patchy, local knowledge was vital. Still, it started my love affair with Ireland.

It was around then that poles started to become fashionable, and for me it was love at first sight. I'd used a few of the early ones, including a green Lerc with an action like a hosepipe at 7 m. But now the first carbon poles came in. I bought a 'double mono carbon' pole; it was 10 m and was the most expensive pole available. You could hardly hold it, let alone fish with it at full length. Eight metres was as long as you could handle. I was delighted with it and that pole was to stand me in good stead when I first went to Northern Ireland.

Ray Mumford was the only angler who had really foreseen the potential of the pole, but he was fishing on a different circuit to me, and anyway, he was so secretive that I couldn't get near him. I was frightened to talk to him. I tried once and I never tried again. Micky Thill was very keen on pole fishing, and owned an old cane Sowerbutts pole, but there were no really good pole anglers to watch or talk to.

Then I went to see a roadshow starring Ian Heaps at Essex University in Colchester. Ian had just won the World Championship, then gone to Ireland and smashed the world record with a roach catch of 166 lb 11 oz 8 dr (75.62 kg). Everything was going right for him at the time, and he puts things over very well. I was fascinated as he talked through how he had used special floats and why, and discussed some techniques on pole fishing that he had picked up from watching the Continentals at the World Championships. I came home and made some big pole floats straight away. I actually used one of my home-made specials when I just missed out on beating Ian's record.

Listening to Ian at the roadshow had made me determined to try Northern Ireland. In the late 1970s there was an explosion of roach on the River Erne system and they drew people like a magnet. The premier match then was the Benson & Hedges, and it became so popular that a couple of years later there was a draw for the tickets. I've fished it every year since 1978.

In that first year I went with Peter, and we stayed in the Lakeland Hotel, just outside Enniskillen. It's now an old people's home. On the river, you could see roach topping everywhere. There had been a lot of rain, so the river had a bit of pace but all week the weather was beautiful. It was so warm that Kevin Ashurst went swimming. I didn't really know him then. He was my hero, and I was frightened even to talk to him. I'd heard these stories about how sharp he was.

I had prepared very carefully for the match, which takes place on alternate days. As the feed went in and the fish came on to it, fishing got better and better through the week. That's why a lot of other match organizers, such as Cliff Smart and Keith Boswell, took on the idea of running a similar formula competition on the weeks following the main festival.

Because you couldn't buy the heavy floats needed, I'd made all my own. My rigs weren't very good; I was using lead olivettes stopped with shot on the line. This is exactly the wrong way to set up when you're going to catch a lot of fish, because those shot are bumping up and down, and gradually wearing loose. Ian had advised us to use big-eyed hooks, so we could grab hold of them more easily. He thought they were better because they didn't cut your hands as badly as a spade-end hook. You could always tell when someone had taken a big bag of fish. Their palm and fingers were a mass of cuts.

I was really looking forward to the fishing, especially as the float didn't stop going under when I practised. Fortunately I had a good draw on the first day at Rosscarne, and came third in my section. I weighed in 61 lb (27.66 kg) of roach, which was the best roach catch I had ever had. Nowadays, with the modern poles and improved techniques, I would have had more than 100 lb (45 kg), but then I was chuffed as could be. I used my new carbon pole at 7 metres, fishing to hand and feeding heavily with groundbait and maggot. It was flowing quite hard, but the peg was 7 ft (2.1 m) deep. And there were so many fish there. I still had a wicker basket in those days, and I got caught up in the social drinking that is a big part of a week's fishing in Northern Ireland. Nowadays, I'm not one for staying up late if I have a big match the following day. That said, it doesn't seem to have affected Kevin!

On the second match two days later, I drew the dreaded H section at Schools. Over recent years, this has become a no-hope section, but there were so many fish in

the river that year, there was the chance of a few fish anywhere – as Kevin was to prove in the last match when he drew Schools and weighed in more than 100 lb (45 kg) on the final day.

My peg looked a real duff one. It was shallow close in, with no flow, and the float was obviously out of the question. I hadn't been in Ireland long, but I knew enough to work out that my only hope was the lead. So I fished the feeder with worm and caster on the hook to take 56 lb 13 oz (25.8 kg) of bream. It put me second in the section, and I was 22nd overall with one match to go. I thought that with a good draw on the final day, I even had an outside chance of finishing in the top five. But I didn't get a good draw – I got a brilliant one.

I've always had a reputation for turning up late. It's because I'm always fiddling about getting bits of tackle together, running off casters and so on. When we got to the Lakeland Forum, where the match draw was held, there were just four numbers left in the hat. That was Peter, me and two others. I put my hand in and drew out B section, which was the Cornagrade section. It was a great draw almost everywhere, but I picked the plum, B30, the end peg. I knew it was solid with fish.

They were topping everywhere. The swim was on a landing-stage and was 6 ft (1.8 m) deep but dead level, and I didn't have to go any further out than 5 metres. I caught from the very start and it was one of the most fantastic day's fishing that I've had. The fish were there all the time and I caught 498, nearly all roach but a few bream and hybrids. I nearly always count my fish because it enables me to get into a rhythm, and to tell if my catch rate is slowing. Anglers who find this difficult should practise on low-catch waters and gradually build up.

I used a 14 ft (4.25 m) green Garbolino fibre-glass pole, with a float that was really too light at about 4 g, and a size 10 hook with four or five maggots. I just kept cramming on another maggot when the used ones became too sucked. My hand was cut to ribbons by that big hook. At least I had nipped off the barb so that I could unhook quickly. Even at that stage, I was aware of the need to unhook with the hand holding the pole for speed. Any angler who is still putting down his rod or pole and switching to his main hand to unhook will never be able to take really big weights. You have to practise catching the fish with one hand and unhooking with the other, the one that's holding the rod or pole, when you're swinging fish to hand.

I kept the fish coming with loads of groundbait – about 20 lb (90 kg) of dry. Ian had told us how to do this, mixing it in the big maggot trays used by bait breeders. He had a catchphrase: 'The more you throw at them, the more you catch'. It really was true.

I knew I had a lot of fish, but I had no idea what weight I had. I certainly didn't know I was 2 oz (56 g) off Ian's world record. Just one more fish in the net would have done it. On those jetties, you inevitably have quite a few fish that fall off behind you. It's generally quicker to get the bait out again rather than get up and collect the fish, which always bounces back into the water just as you're going to grab it.

I can't remember how many weighs I had, but it was about six. I've always been good with figures and suddenly it hit me: 'This isn't far off the record.' And it wasn't – 166 lb 9 oz 8 dr (75.56 kg). Just one fish . . . It wouldn't have stood as a world record for very long, even if I had caught a couple more fish. The next year my team-mate Dennis Willis became the first angler to take over 200 lb (90 kg) in a match, and shortly after that, Pete Burrell had 258 lb 9 oz 8 dr (75.56 kg) off the Sillees river. And it didn't make any difference to my angling career. That catch was probably the most important in my life.

The angling press were caught on the hop. They all rushed round to interview me afterwards, but they had missed out on pictures. Who was Bob Nudd, anyway? Nobody had heard of me. The following day I had to go to the peg again, which wasn't much of a hardship, and simulate it for them because they didn't have any pictures. There were two terrific reports in *Angling Times* and *Angler's Mail*, a few days later, and another big piece in the *Daily Mirror* about this unknown company director from Chelmsford. And that's the absolute truth. I was unknown, completely unknown.

The catch pushed me up to second overall with 276 lb 9 oz (125.44 kg), which was worth £1,400, my biggest win at the time. But Kevin got the top money. He showed just how brilliant he is by taking more than 300 lb (135 kg) over the three days.

Looking back, with the knowledge I have now, I should probably have beaten even Pete Burrell's 258 lb (140.25 kg) catch that he made from the Sillees river a couple of years later. I got the feeding about right, but how I would love to turn back the clock and be there with today's poles, floats, hooks and line! I still think it was a very good catch in the circumstances, because I had experienced just one day of catching fish like that beforehand.

As if I wasn't on a big enough high after coming so close to smashing the world record, I came back to England and immediately won a big match on the Lea. It was a rotten weight, 1 lb 5 oz (590 g) of little bleak and roach, but Dennis Salmon was there as a bookie and I won £600. I don't even think that I fished terribly well, but suddenly I had two successes in two weeks and won £2,000. I went out and bought a new pole, spent some on clothes and gave the rest to my wife. I thought: 'I'm on my way now.'

And suddenly, it seemed I was. The confidence that those two matches had given me made all the difference. Until then, I had won just one open. Now, I was starting to figure regularly in the prize money, and winning quite a few. And when I went back to Northern Ireland in 1979, I did well even though I didn't draw any real fliers. Over the three days I weighed in 181 lb 12 oz 8 dr (82.45 kg), good enough for seventh overall. But I had to wait another two years before I won my first event, as distinct from a day prize, on the Erne.

In 1980 I first started to talk to Kevin, though I think it was Peter Clapperton who actually broke the ice. Kevin is a great socializer, and so is Peter, so it was inevitable that they would get chatting one evening. I had to wait another year before I got to know him well. That was when I won the Bass-Fermanagh Championships, one of those matches held after the Benson & Hedges. Actually, it wasn't all that spectacular a victory, because everybody cleared off after the big festival week. There were so few fishing that everybody could get on Cornagrade. I won and Kevin was second. We both caught hybrids up in the water, but I beat him by 56 lb (25.4 kg) to 52 lb (23.58 kg). There weren't many bream around, and the roach had gone by then. They come into the river from Lough Erne to spawn, and within a couple of weeks, they are gone.

At first I travelled to Enniskillen only for the Benson & Hedges, but I was soon staying for two weeks, then three, then four. Other match organizers cottoned on that if weather conditions were unfavourable and the roach weren't in for the Benson's, they would turn up soon afterwards. There seemed to be a run of bad weather for about four years, which meant that the better fishing was actually after the Benson's I took lots of 100 lb (45 kg) bags, both roach and bream. My biggest catch at that time was just over 200 lb (90 kg).

In fact, I was in line to break the world record on another occasion. That was when Pete Burrell had 258 lb (140.25 kg) from the Sillees river, an offshoot of the Erne that was so tiny you could touch the far bank on most of it with a 10 m pole.

I fished that match and drew about 10 pegs from Pete, who also fished for Essex County at the time. I had the most incredible first hour, taking about 70 lb (31.75 kg), with roach coming as fast as I could catch them. If they had kept feeding like that, I would have had 300 lb (135 kg) easily. But they moved along the river and I couldn't get a bite. There was just nothing left in my peg. Pete, who had a slightly deeper peg, kept them coming all day. But it was a privilege to be there and see that huge catch.

In the early 1980s things were going very well for me in Ireland, but I was still relatively unknown in English match circles. All that started to change however, as I became more involved with Essex County, and Catpack effectively merged with Essex County. Not only did we have one of the strongest sides in the country, but we had one of the shrewdest managers in Dennis Salmon. If Dick Clegg hadn't become England manager, Dennis would have done a very good job.

In the first year that he took over, we won the Captain Morgan Cup, a nationwide knockout competition with teams of 12. Although it was billed as the FA Cup of fishing, small teams really didn't have much of a chance. They might be able to beat a stronger team if they got a home draw, but the final was bound to be between two good teams because you needed a squad of all-round anglers to handle the different waters. Later on, with some different sponsors, there were some terrific foreign venues for the final, but the year we won it, the final was held on Worksop middle lake, a horrible venue with a dam going over it. There were a few fish on peg 1, but it got worse as you got further from the dam. Fortunately Tommy Boulton was on peg 1 by the dam, and won it for us with 4 lb 4 oz 8 dr (1.95 kg) of small roach. But 14 of us in a line didn't have a bite, and only eight out of the 24 caught fish. It was a pretty poor choice for such an important final, but at least we won it, and £3,000, beating Isaak Walton Preston by 5 lb 10 oz (2.55 kg) to 2 lb 12 oz (1.25 kg). Dennis's influence was a key factor in our success. In those days there were all sorts of strokes being pulled, and you had to be very sharp to keep ahead of the game. One team took us on a water that just had pike in it, and wouldn't let us practise there. But Dennis got round it, and we won anyway.

Dennis also masterminded our victory in the Division 1 National Championship on the River Ancholme, near Scunthorpe in 1981, the first victory by a southern-based team in the event. We'd been up there for two weeks practising. Dennis was very keen on practice to sort out a method, and he was very hard on those who didn't or couldn't make it. To show commitment to the team, you had to turn up on those practices. Nowadays such a thing

is standard, but then it was pretty revolutionary to take the whole squad on to a water for two weeks. But that was Dennis, a great thinker. He brought a professional approach to the side.

Anyway, Dennis had picked up this method from Billy Knott senior, whose Marazion team had done very well the year before with it. It consisted of using little balls of groundbait with squatts across the river, as for bream, but with the same mix on the inside for roach and skimmers. The secret was to feed very carefully.

Like most Nationals, the water fished far worse on the day than it had in practice, but our method still worked. We had one blank – Micky Thill – but the fishing was very hard and we had such a consistent performance that the dry net didn't matter. To make things even better for us, our strongest bream anglers, Jimmy Randall and Tommy Boulton, drew in sections where there were a few bream. To win the National Championship, you need a bit of luck. It worked for us that day, with our big-fish anglers in the right places, and the small fish experts like Billy Hughes and myself in areas where we could scratch out a few fish.

In those days, it took ages to work out the results because it was all done manually. Tenth, ninth, eighth and so on down to third. We knew we had done well, but other teams were claiming a lot of points too. When they read out Scunthorpe, we were really excited because we knew we were at least second. And when they called out Warrington as runner-up we went berserk. We had beaten the best teams in the country by a clear 26 points.

I was fifth in my section with 2 lb 9 oz 2 dr (1.65 kg), and it's the only time I've ever been in a winning National team. I was only beaten by anglers who had big bream. There were about 40 blanks in my section, and the method worked perfectly for me. I had several skimmers of about 5 oz (140 g) each and a couple of roach. The National is one of the few major individual titles that I have never won, and I would love to, not just because it's worth about £10,000, but also because it has a very special atmosphere.

These days, there is no difference between the top southern and northern anglers, but 10 years ago there was quite a big divide. We certainly weren't the best team there that day. We just had that vital bit of luck. I was very aware of my own inadequacies when I watched anglers like Ivan Marks, Kevin Ashurst and the best of the Barnsley team. Even a young Tommy Pickering seemed to be brilliant at all sorts of methods.

The great thing about the National win was that it meant we qualified for the World Club Team Championships,

Dennis Salmon who died in 1993. A brilliant team captain, he won all the open honours but would have loved to have captained England.

which in 1983 were held on the River Arno in Florence. Dennis insisted that all those in the running for the team should spend 10 days over there familiarizing themselves with the river. This was my first real trip abroad (you can't really count Ireland) and I thought Italy, and especially Florence, was wonderful. I met a lot of people from that trip who are still close friends. We certainly needed someone who understood a little English, because none of us understood any Italian!

The Arno is terrific fishing. There were some chub, even a few goldfish, but carp looked likely to be the main attack. I love carp. They have won me loads of matches, and I believe that they will be the fish of the future too. They are ravenous feeders, terrific fighters and grow quickly – a fishery owner's dream and an angler's, too. I had been very lucky to learn about carp in the 1970s, before specialist small carp fisheries were even considered. and the water where I got my education was Layer Pits in Colchester.

CARP FISHING

It was the hot summer of 1976 that turned Layer from an ordinary fishery into a great one. There were carp in there, but we never caught them in any real numbers until 1976, when I walked around the water in the summer. I'd heard that it was fishing well, with millions of 2 oz (56 g) carp to be caught. I have never seen anything like it since. It was as if there was a black cloud in the water, and they were all carp, millions and millions of them. We started off fishing with 3- and 4-m whips, groundbait and maggots, and caught 30-40 lb (13.6-18.15 kg) of them.

The following year they were too big for that. We just kept getting broken if we tried to whip them out. So we caught them instead on the pole with paste, just over the edge of the shelf. The year following that they all moved out of the margins. That's when we switched to legering for them, feeding groundbait and using quivertips. We had learnt about floating maggots from Ivan Marks, which proved a devastating method. There were so many fish from that wonderful breeding year that we went to every open we could. Winning catches were sometimes as high as 120 lb (54.45 kg). But each year you could see these fish getting bigger and bigger, and demanding a different approach to catch them. It went from fishing the whip close in to a short pole with elastic, then to the bomb, and finally, floats capable of casting up to 100 yd (m).

Some great years on that water taught me a few essential lessons about carp fishing, and gave me the confidence

to play big fish on very light tackle. For example, I learnt never to strike on carp. When that tip goes right round, it isn't because the carp has hold of the bait, it's because it knows the hook is in its mouth and it's hooked. If you strike at such bites, you're asking to be broken, especially on light tackle. All you need to do is lift up and backwind.

Although some anglers just fished with a quivertip in those days, I liked to use a butt indicator. I could point the rod dead straight to where I was fishing, so when the carp took off, the reel would backwind more easily than if it was at an angle. It also helped because we were feeding heavily. We didn't have to keep looking away while we were feeding. One minute we'd be looking at a motionless indicator, the next it would be banging against the rod.

The carp had got pretty smart and we had to cast quite a way for them. One-ounce (28 g) bombs were needed to reach them, and 6-8 ft (1.8-2.45 m) tails. We used 13 ft (3.95 m) match rods to cast with such a long tail. This was because we caught a lot of fish on the drop. We would be feeding balls of groundbait, and the carp were coming up in the water. When they take like that, they really hit hard. With so many fish to try new methods on, we refined our methods and tackle. But always the secret was to feed, feed, feed. Sometimes we would take 25 lb (11.35 kg) of groundbait, and the only time we didn't put that much in was when we were in a good peg playing fish all day. If we weren't playing fish, we were feeding them.

Years of that sort of fishing taught me a lot about feeding groundbait accurately and the need to fix a marker in order to drop it in the same spot every time. This became easier when we started using floats, because then we could see that we were feeding in the right spot. It's very easy to be a little bit out on the lead. That's really why we started using floats. They gave us an added advantage; we could pull the float back into the feed. With carp it generally pays to twitch a bait, anyway.

We developed floats that took about 1 oz (30 g). We couldn't buy floats like that so we made our own, mostly with black tops. There was an eye in the bottom of the float, but it wasn't possible to hold such a float with SSGs because the pressure of casting was so great. Instead, we used large leger stops clipped either side of the float. There was no weight down the line at all. We fitted 5 lb (2.25 kg) shock leaders to take the strain of casting. When a fish took, the float usually just lifted a bit, and then it was gone. By then the reel was backwinding.

The hook length was usually 2 lb (900 g) Maxima and hooks were size 20 or 22 90340s baited with a couple of floating maggots or sinkers. This is a barbless hook and that's very important for carp fishing, because when you are playing one, it's going one way, then the other. That hook is twisting as the fish turns, goes down and comes up. If you've got a barbed hook, the barb gradually enlarges the hole in its mouth and eventually will probably come free. With a barbless hook it doesn't matter if it rotates, because the hole stays the same size. I don't use 90340s now. The quality of hooks has improved so I use Browning 354s and nip the barb off.

I still prefer small hooks, though. Carp are strange fish. Even in those days of plenty, 20s and 22s produced more fish. The finer the hook, the finer the line and the more

bites we got. There's a balance between being able to get them in and not having quite so many bites. The 20 or 22 fits neatly in the middle.

Layer also taught me about mixing groundbaits and stimulating fish, particularly carp, into feeding. It was a wonderful education because it has made me aggressive in my fishing. I'm not by nature a cautious angler, and if there are a lot of fish around, that suits me fine. In those days I saved all my old casters and put them in my fridge open so they became floaters. I used to take 1 gallon (4.5 litres) of casters to every match and crush them up, along with 5-6 lb (2.25-2.7 kg) of hemp and some pinkies. We needed a fairly stiffish mix to get that lot out and generally used just

Even at this size, carp will grab a sizeable bait.

brown and white crumb. If I ever ran into similar fishing, I'd probably use some continental groundbait, but 50 per cent would still be brown crumb.

The most important lesson in preparing groundbait to put out that sort of distance is that it must be mixed thoroughly beforehand and allowed to soak. In other words, don't mix it two minutes before you are going to start firing it out. Mix it as soon as you get to your peg, let it dry out a bit and add more water until you get the right consistency. I don't usually worry about riddling it with that sort of volume.

Another big lesson from those days was in playing carp. I learnt that patience is needed. Don't try and force them, particularly when they are right under your feet. I've seen anglers play a carp patiently for 20 minutes, get it under their feet, put an extra bit of pressure on and the hook comes out. That's 20 minutes wasted. The first thing is never to strike, just pick the rod up and start to backwind. Carp nearly always run away from you. Let a carp finish its first run, then wind into it and start to bring it in steadily. As soon as it runs again, let it. If there are no obstructions, you will be surprised how large a fish you can land on 2 lb (1 kg) line. And every matchman should backwind rather than play a fish off the clutch.

The biggest carp I landed at Layer weighed 14 lb (6.35 kg), but one of my friends, Bob Cheeseman, had one of 28 lb 8 oz (12.9 kg). The best match weight I had was 130 lb, (58.95 kg), and that was with only 20 fish.

I never did much pole fishing at Layer, but I learnt a lot about playing fish and how carp responded to feed, so I've always had an advantage with the advent of specialist carp match-fisheries. They all seem to have different techniques of feeding and you have to find out whether they want loose feed or groundbait. Usually, it's a matter of the distance at which you can catch. Often this is out of range of loose feed. Many carp waters ban groundbait anyway. However, I think carp will come to any feed eventually. Whether it's caster, maggot or groundbait, you have to keep something happening to keep them interested. Eventually they will find your feed and start feeding.

Once a carp gets over 7 lb (3.15 kg), it is difficult to handle on a pole unless you can use really big hooks and thick lines. However, a pole allows you to present a bait perfectly and use a very small float. Carp are crafty and you have to strike at bites more on a pole, rather than waiting for the float to disappear. The elastic provides a cushion, allowing you to do this. You must put on pressure immediately to turn or stop the fish. The idea is to slow a fish before it can develop too much speed.

Even with a No. 8 elastic through three sections, it doesn't take a carp long to reach the point when the elastic 'bottoms out', that is, when there's no more stretch in it. Then you're in trouble! You need extra sections ready to hand, and it takes a while to learn to add them smoothly. Those extra sections can give another 3-4 metres. The fish is running against heavy pressure and sometimes that extra length is just enough to turn it. Once you have slowed and stopped the fish, you really need to create more pressure, but you can't. It would be lovely to have an elastic that's a bit soft to start with, and increases its tension the further that a fish runs.

Leicester tackle-dealer Roy Marlow recently showed me a system with catapult elastic that acts like a bungee strap. He had thick catapult elastic through the bottom section of the pole, so he had three sections of normal elastic and a fourth with catapult elastic. It couldn't be

EXPERIMENTAL CARP RIG COMBINING NO. 8 ELASTIC WITH CATAPULT ELASTIC

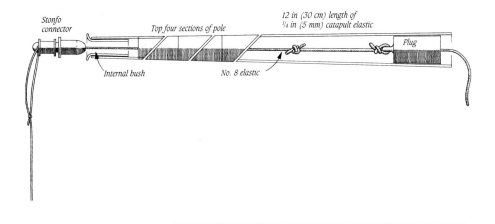

Stonfo connector

Top four sections of pole

12 in (30 cm) length of ¼ in (5 mm) catapult elastic

Plug

Internal bush

No. 8 elastic

bottomed out by the fish because it was too strong, but it could still stretch quite a way. It would probably give a couple of extra yards, and it couldn't give that 'dead' feeling that fully stretched elastic gives. I like the idea and I'll be experimenting with it.

Ideally, you want to use the heaviest line and hook you can get away with. I won the ACA Masters at Mallory Park in 1992, and I had 44 lb (19.95 kg) of carp on 0.16 main line and a size 14 hook. The biggest carp I took was 5 lb 8 oz (2.5 kg). It was one of those days when I knew there were lots of carp about, and I knew that I could get them on heavy line. I caught a few biggish roach and bits fishing close in and loosefeeding. However, I wasn't catching very well, so I went out on a 10 m line, still loosefeeding. Ken Giles, the Shakespeare team captain, was next to me and struggling as well. He started putting in an occasional ball of groundbait, and hooked a carp. Then he got another one. I copied Kenny's feeding pattern, putting in a ball every cast, and ended up with 44 lb (19.95 kg) to his 29 lb (13.15 kg).

There are several fisheries now that demand a lot of feed, perhaps 1 gallon of maggots. Heyford Fisheries, near Daventry, is one and Priory Farm, near Gatwick, is another. Steve Gardener used to run matches down there. The carp were only 10 oz-1 lb (283-450 g), but we had to fish very light for them – a 22 hook and 12 oz (0.25 kg) bottoms. You just cast out with a light waggler with no shot down the line in 8-10 ft (2.45-3m) of water, and all of a sudden you were backwinding. If you fished 1½ lb (0.75 kg) bottoms, you never got a bite. I was taking 50 lb (22.7 kg) weights on 12 oz (0.25 kg) bottoms.

Fishing waters like that teaches you to feed while you're still playing a fish. I learnt this from Layer, where it could take 20 minutes to land a fish. You had to clamp the rod between your legs, sometimes even lay it down, put two more balls of groundbait in and pick the rod up again.

My standard approach for carp in summer is always to fish the top. Virtually no shot on the line, small hooks, light line (as long as there are no obstructions near by) and fishing maggot but feeding caster. I think carp react better to something that moves. Red is my favourite maggot colour, though fluorescent pinkies are brilliant too.

On the pole, I always use a high-tech line. On rod and line, I want a line with some stretch so I use Browning or Maxima. When I fished the 1989 World Championships in Bulgaria, I caught during practice using thick flick tips with 5 lb (2.5 kg) Maxima direct. I was hauling 5 lb (2.25 kg) carp out in seconds. It's really amazing how quickly you can get them out.

I know several matchmen who use boilies for carp, but I don't. I stick to the baits I know. Worms, cheese and boilies will all catch carp, but you need to have confidence in what you're doing. I wouldn't have that confidence if I put on a boilie!

THE WORLD'S BEST TEAM

And certainly on that day on the Arno in 1983, in the World Club Team Championships, boilies were no part of our team plan! The match stretch was only about 7 ft (2.45 m) deep, but very slow-moving. It called for waggler fishing, largely because we didn't have the quality of poles that are around nowadays, and anyway, English anglers in those days really had to go for bigger fish to be able to compete with the best Continental sides.

The most important part of our team plan was to feed little balls of sticky maggot in order to get clumps of bait down to the bottom and give the carp something to feed on. If you loosefed, you were pestered by lots of tiny fish that were very difficult to hook. So the feed had to be on or near the bottom.

The problem lay in keeping a hooked carp in your zone. The match was fished to World Championship rules, which meant that if a fish ran outside your designated 15 metres, it was disqualified. But as everyone knows, once carp are hooked they just charge off and you can't stop them. We had to conceal where a hooked fish was by pushing the rod right under the water. It's difficult for an angler to know where the fish is, but it's impossible for a steward or onlooker to say that the fish is out of your zone. At first the carp just ran out, and we were backwinding. Then we pushed the rod right under the water, and kept it there until the fish was almost beaten. It was another smart piece of thinking by Dennis, and it was to prove absolutely essential.

Matches in Italy, especially during the summer, start early because it gets so hot during the day. We had the draw at 6 am and the three-hour match started at 8 am. A big contest on the Arno is quite an experience. There is a 30 ft (10 m) wall behind you, with thousands of Italians sitting on top. I'd never seen so many people at a match before. There must have been 20,000, and they were all expecting the Italian team to win.

I used a 22 with single maggot and made sure I had a couple of bleak early on so that I was sure to weigh in. All the time I was feeding little balls of sticky maggot about four rod-lengths out. The carp tackle was a bit different: 3 lb (1.5 kg) main line and 2 lb (1 kg) hooklength to a size 18 forged hook and double maggot. After about 30 minutes, it was time to try for them.

I started on the heavy gear, feeding the sticky maggot and hoping. After about 20 minutes I hooked a carp. I didn't strike: you hardly ever need to with carp. I soon had my rod under the water. It was driving the Italians crazy because they couldn't see what was happening, except that I had a fish on. By then the carp was already three parts across the river, and it seemed to take an eternity getting the fish back to me. I was praying that it didn't snag anybody else's line. It took 20 minutes, but my experience of catching carp at Layer pits proved invaluable. I knew when I had got the fish beaten. It was about 4 lb (1.8 kg), and was the biggest fish caught in the match.

That was my section win straight away. I was miles in front then, and I could now relax and fish for individual glory. Not that it made any difference. I would have been fishing the same way anyway.

I only had to wait another 20 minutes before the float went away again. The fish did the same thing – headed for

the far bank and I pushed my rod under the water, but this one didn't play the game. It ran along rather than out, and soon there were two other anglers playing the fish as well! They got it in, but it was disqualified because they could see it was on my line. With two hours of the match gone, I had another fish, of about 3 lb (1.35 kg). Once again my experience at Layer made the difference. Don't strike, let it run, take your time and keep that rod right under the water. Put pressure on when it's close to get its head up, but be ready to backwind all the time. It came in safely, and though I had no more carp, I got a chub about 12 oz (340 g) near the end.

Dennis and our two runners told me that I had won my section, but I didn't know I had taken the individual title. I weighed in 9 lb 11 oz 8 dr (4.5 kg), which won it quite easily. As if that wasn't enough, we won the team match too, the first and only English team ever to do so. Our worst result was Micky Thill, who was fifth in his section. Tommy Boulton was second, Bob Cheeseman third, so we had beaten the Italians on their home patch.

When there are very big carp around, it's best to change to a running line.

Me in the early 1980s with a good net of roach.

The evening presentation was the most memorable occasion of my life. The food was fabulous, wine was flowing and there were masses of trophies, badges and medals. I was given this beautiful bronze fish statuette, which is one of the best trophies I have ever won. I've won so many trophies that it's hard to know where to put them all, but that one gets pride of place in my workroom.

That evening gave me something else too: an introduction to a lot of the Italian methods. During our time over there, I had made friends with two Italians, Andre Collini and Franco Miccinesi, who had a tackle shop. They're now the bosses of Colmic, which is one of the largest makers of Italian tackle.

I brought back a load of Italian gear, especially bleak whips, styl leads and those wonderfully made little Italian pole floats that were almost impossible to get in England. The Italians are so generous with their tackle. They never charged me and I wanted to do something for them, but they always seem to have everything, and in most cases a lot better than we had.

The Italian tackle and methods gave me a valuable edge. One place that proved a happy hunting ground for me was Billericay Lakes, where there were a lot of evening matches. Using a whip, you could catch up to 10 lb (4.5 kg) of roach off the surface in a three-hour contest. I wasn't that good at it, but once I had been to Italy and seen where I was going wrong, I adapted my methods and rigs, and really started to win some money there.

Most of all, I had been fascinated with the Italian bleaking methods (see page 17). I came back and used the same set-up on the Lea, and won four matches in a row on bleak. I even learnt how to hook a maggot from the Italians. I'm not talking about ordinary roach fishing but situations like bleaking or gudgeon fishing, where you want to take several fish on the same maggot. Milo Colombo, who's been a regular member of the Italian team for the past 10 years, showed me how to do it.

It takes a little practice to get it right, because you use the movement of the maggot to work the hook round. It has to be threaded right inside the maggot from the blunt end, with the hook coming out at the pointed end. The Italians breed specially hard maggots and pinkies that don't get crushed easily by the fish. I had learnt how to handle fish quickly, but I learnt from Milo that I was striking wrong. In the end, it's all down to rhythm, because the Italians hardly strike at all.

I was fishing a lake in Palma, where there were quite a few bleak, with Milo, and watching how he did it. 'Now you have a go,' he said. I wasn't aware that I was catching that fast, because when you have a good rhythm, it never seems that quick. But Milo said: 'Do you know how many fish you've had in the past minute?' I thought he would say four or five. I was astonished when he told me I had caught nine. If you could keep that rate up, it would be more than 500 an hour, which is what some of the best Italians can achieve when they're on fish. It is just a matter of getting the bait, the tackle and the rhythm right. That said, I've never been able to repeat it in England, though I'd like to have a go at those big shoals of bleak on the Wye.

The Italian bleaking rig is very different from that used by most people in England. The Italians use four very small styl leads, with the closest often only 1 in (2.5 cm) or so from the hook. The set-up shows immediately if a bleak has taken. The floats are very small and delicate. I'd worked that out, but what I was doing wrong was using lines like Bayer or Maxima. The Italians taught me that it's vital to use the pre-stretched, high-tech lines. When you are using a tiny float, you must couple it with a fine line. Try this for yourself. Set up a 4 × No.10 float and put on 2 lb (1 kg) Maxima. You will really strain to cast it. Now put on 0.06 line and you can flick it out easily.

The World Club Team Championships played a big part in making me better known. After all, beating the Italians on their home patch had never been done before. I got a lot of publicity, and it played a very big part in being picked for my first home international. I think Kevin, who was highly respected by Stan Smith, put a good word in for me too.

At that time I had never thought about fishing for England, even in the home internationals, until the phone rang at home one evening in 1983. It was Stan Smith. He had a very gruff voice and just said: 'I want you to fish in the home international. Can you make it?' Of course I said yes. I was terrified of Stan, and frightened even to talk to him. I certainly didn't chat to him about what it would be like!

The match was on Loch Kilbirnie. We could fish either waggler or a pole, but it was too shallow close in for a pole, or at least for a pole at the lengths we had then. Waggler was the only method, because the competition was fished to World Championship rules, which ban legering. Fortunately it was easy fishing. There were plenty of good roach there, up to 8 oz (225 g), that responded to groundbait. I fished the waggler and won my section with 21 lb (9.5 kg).

It put me fifth overall, and I started to think that there might be a chance of making the full England squad for the World Championships. Then Stan Smith was replaced by a new manager, Dick Clegg, whom I didn't know very well, was chosen. I thought that my chance of fishing for England in the World Championships had disappeared. 'Ah well,' I thought, 'at least I've fished for England, even if it was only in a home international.' But Dick Clegg knew a lot more about me than I realized.

3

MAN OF THE WORLD

*I*had never really thought about fishing in the World Championships. Even getting picked for a home international was a real honour, and when Stan Smith was sacked as England manager, it looked unlikely that I would fish another home international, let alone get a call-up for the full England squad. I was in Northern Ireland around the end of May 1984, fishing the Cliff Smart series of matches, when I got a telephone call from Dick Clegg, the new England team manager. I had met him occasionally, but I didn't know him very well. What I didn't know was that Dick had been out to Switzerland to look at the World Championship venue, and found it was pole fishing to hand. I had built up a reasonable reputation for pole fishing to hand on the Wensum and in Ireland, but I had not the remotest idea that I was even in the running for an England slot.

Pole fishing to hand for
bream in Ireland.

I can't remember exactly what his words were. Dick is usually quite abrupt until you get to know him, and he just said: 'I want you to make yourself available for practice for the World Championships in Switzerland. Will you be available?' Of course I said yes. I felt fantastic. It was unbelievable: I was actually in the England squad. Of course he didn't say I was in the team, but just being part of the side was enough. At the time there was still a lot of north-south rivalry, and a lot of people had talked about how a Barnsley man would never pick any southerners. Some even said that I was the token southerner, and that I had no chance of getting in the team itself.

The squad that year was Kevin Ashurst, Denis White, Tommy Pickering, Ian Heaps, Alan McAtee and myself. Ian and I went over beforehand to have a look at the venue, the River Thielle at Yverdon. I piled every bit of tackle I had into my car, picked up Ian and off we went. We took a lot of maggots with us, loaded in polystyrene boxes.

TRANSPORTING BAIT

If you're transporting maggots abroad, the best way is to collect them from a bait farm or tackle shop chilled right down. Try to buy them without too much sawdust. I generally just put a little maize with mine. Put about 3 gallons in a black bin liner, remove all the air and seal it up. Then put the bin liner in a polystyrene container or cold box, squashing the maggots in tight, and seal it up with a couple of bottles of ice.

Don't bother with those cold packs; they only last about six hours whereas a 4 pt (2 litre) water bottle will keep your bait perfect for at least 30 hours. The main thing to remember is that this needs to be done quickly. You don't want the maggots wriggling around when you seal them. Then seal your polystyrene container or cold box with tape. The last thing you want is to drop it and have 3 gallons (13.5 litre) of maggots on a boat deck or in a plane hold! It's a great way to carry them because you have none of the smell usually associated with several gallons of maggots.

When you open them, they all look dead. The longer they have been sealed, the longer they take to come round. After an hour, one or two are moving and it may take five or six hours for the lot to revive. Remember to take large trays to keep them in, and if you're leaving them outdoors, make sure you have something to cover them.

Casters are more difficult to transport because they deteriorate more rapidly. They still last two or three days if you transport them in a similar way, but seal them in thick polythene so you don't get any burns on them from

the ice packs. As soon as you get to your destination, put them in cold water, and change the water every day. When transporting worms, you have to be very careful because they will get out of any container you put them in. You have to seal the lid with a fine mesh and a tight elastic band. Don't chill worms down at all, and don't keep them totally in the dark, but somewhere where there is some light on them. If there is light they won't come out, but as soon as it is dark they want to escape! And don't put in just worms on their own. You need a big bucket with some of the natural feed that has been in there: manure, grass, moss or whatever waste they were bred in. At the end of the journey, pick out any that are dead because these will soon kill off the rest.

You can transport bloodworm and joker in very much the same way as maggots. First, make sure the joker is perfectly dry. Wrap it in newspaper, fold the paper up and roll it into a coil. Then put it into a polystyrene container.

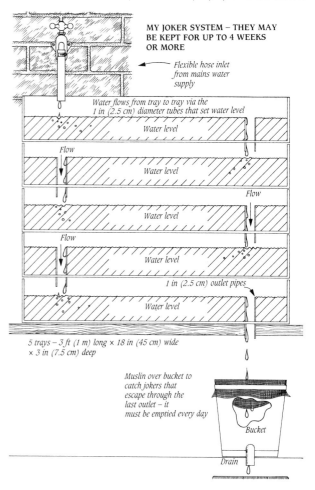

MY JOKER SYSTEM – THEY MAY BE KEPT FOR UP TO 4 WEEKS OR MORE

Flexible hose inlet from mains water supply

Water flows from tray to tray via the 1 in (2.5 cm) diameter tubes that set water level

Water level

Flow

Water level

Flow

Water level

Flow

Water level

1 in (2.5 cm) outlet pipes

Water level

5 trays – 3 ft (1 m) long × 18 in (45 cm) wide × 3 in (7.5 cm) deep

Muslin over bucket to catch jokers that escape through the last outlet – it must be emptied every day

Bucket

Drain

You can stand these coils on end and fit lots in. Don't pile them on top of one another, because there should be no weight on top of them. Put in a couple of iced bottles to keep them cool, seal the polystyrene container and they will keep for two or three days. Don't open the container to check on the joker because you need to prevent air getting into it. When you open the rolled paper, the joker will be perfect, though they take a little while to come round. Joker is always best used fresh, and if you keep it for four days without an aquarium, you've done brilliantly.

You need to be a little more careful with bloodworm because it dies if it gets too cold, but you can run it through a maggot riddle once you get to your destination. The dead ones are left on top of the riddle. Then repack them in clean paper. I do the same for joker, though I use special sacking so I can pour the joker in at one end, tie the top and put it in a tray of water. Muslin is too fine. The holes need to be large enough for the joker to pull through and leave the dead ones behind.

DOING WELL IN SWITZERLAND

Because we knew how to keep our bait, it lasted perfectly well on the journey to Switzerland, though we stopped in Holland to pick up some bloodworm and joker. Neither of us could speak any French or German, but we found out where the match was to be fished and we just went along and set up.

We had been told it was pole fishing to hand, but we soon found out it wasn't. We were soon on long poles and a shortish line in order to get good presentation and run the bait down. Ian is an old campaigner, so I took his advice on the best way to practise. We fished two sessions each day, three hours in the morning and three in the afternoon, and moved around as much as possible. We fished next to one another to simulate match conditions as far as possible. Whenever you fish like this, whether you're practising for a National or a World Championship, you always have to remember that the fishing is always going to be better than in the actual competition. There aren't many people around, nor lots of feed going in, so you invariably catch more fish. On match day, it's never as good as you thought it would be!

Even so, we were able to map out the water pretty well. The top end of the match length was a lot shallower, faster flowing and harder. The middle length was quite good – we caught some chub there – and the bottom end was a bit iffy. We spent a week fishing the river. It was 6-7 ft (1.80-2.15 m) deep and very narrow, but it wasn't easy.

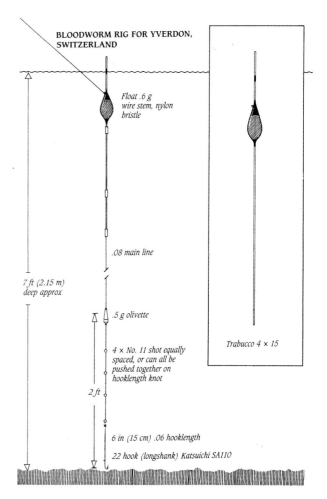

BLOODWORM RIG FOR YVERDON, SWITZERLAND

Float .6 g
wire stem, nylon
bristle

.08 main line

7 ft (2.15 m)
deep approx

.5 g olivette

4 × No. 11 shot equally
spaced, or can all be
pushed together on
hooklength knot

2 ft

6 in (15 cm) .06 hooklength

22 hook (longshank) Katsuichi SA110

Trabucco 4 × 15

Sometimes it was dead still, and at other times it flowed hard. Those pre-practice sessions proved invaluable. We had been told that the Swiss would definitely stop the river for the competition, but on the match, despite all those promises, the river was rushing through. We were later to learn this was just a piece of gamesmanship to deceive the other teams. It certainly made us nearly come unstuck.

Every time the river ran, I could catch dace by putting a float through at a quarter or half pace. The dace turned on every time it flowed, because they like flowing water and it was possible to line them up by putting in little balls loaded with maggots. But when it was still, all you could catch was small perch on bloodworm. I think that week's practice helped me to win a place in the team. I had seen the river in its various moods and knew what fish would respond.

Our official practice was about three weeks later, and about two weeks before the match. If I thought I had worked hard with Ian, I worked twice as hard with Dick driving us. People think it must be fun to fish for England, but it's hard work. They are long, arduous days. Dick gets us up very early in the morning. There are two sessions. If there are six of us fishing, he'll space us out in a certain way and then he'll swap us round. Later, in the evening, we talk about what we have learned and work on rigs.

If it's getting near the end of the week and Dick knows whom he wants in the team – he may have three or four dead certainties – he'll put the two weaker ones together. All the time he's watching what's going on. And we have little private battles between ourselves to catch fish as well. We all experiment and share knowledge, but each has to try to do well himself. Every time you're sitting down, it's like a match. You've got to do as well as you can, even though it's a match where you can't keep any secrets.

Dick didn't say who was in the team when the practice week was over. I didn't really expect to be in, though I did very well in practice. I thought he'd probably go for the experienced anglers. He phoned me about a week after we got back to tell me I was fishing. It was the greatest moment of my life. I felt very excited, but I was aware of the pressure of fishing for England with great anglers like Kevin, Ian, Tommy and Denis, and I was the new boy, very much untried. As it turned out, the key style of fishing was one I knew very well: fishing in flowing water with a pole and holding it back to present a bait at half-speed or slower. But we didn't know that at the time!

We went over a couple of days beforehand to acclimatize, to look at the water, prepare rigs and check our bait. Surprisingly, I slept well on the night before the match. Although I enjoy a drink, there is always so much to do with preparing rigs, tying hooks, checking tackle and so on. You have three hours to fish and everything has to be perfect.

It was a miserable day, grey skies and raining hard, and spectators were on the opposite bank, so on our bank there were just the captains and the press. I can't say I wasn't nervous because I think I was. I knew exactly what the fishing involved, but here I was on the bank, representing my country. It was my first time and I was more worried about letting England down.

I had drawn B section. It was one of the earlier sections and it was a good one. The earlier pegs were shallower and not quite so good, but as you got further down, the depth was more even and there were a few dace to be caught. It was very narrow and rushing through like a torrent. Even in practice we'd never experienced the river moving like this.

Dick assured us: 'The Swiss have told us that it's definitely not going to run. It'll be dead still when the match starts.' I think we'd have won if we had known the truth. Right up to the pre-baiting whistle I was waiting for it to slow down. The biggest float I put up was about 2.5 g, but you needed double that, and it was just a feeling that had made me put on one that big.

I had prepared a light groundbait for feeding with joker, but I had a versatile mix because even if it flowed a little, I still wanted little hard balls to get maggots down to the dace. If it had gone to quarter pace, I could have still used this groundbait but not squeezed it so hard. But it was racing through so hard that it could have done with some stones in it! My pre-baiting feed just wasn't suitable.

When the pre-baiting whistle went five minutes before the match, we all had bait ready for feeding for perch, and the river was still charging through. I thought, 'What am I going to do now?' All my rigs apart from one were useless. Thank goodness we hadn't geared ourselves totally to bloodworm fishing.

I mixed my heavier feed a bit harder and put it closer in, where we expected to catch the perch. But I thought, 'This is obviously not going to be any good,' so I also put some groundbait a little further out, where I thought my dace line would be. I had to adjust very quickly. Had I known what was going to happen, I would have started by feeding groundbait into the middle.

It demanded a quick adjustment. There wasn't time to set up a whole new rig, so I simply put three extra swan shot on my heaviest rig straight away. My experience on flowing waters came to the rescue. If you want to cut the pace down on fast waters to quarter-pace, you need to overshot the float. You're not allowed to have any lead on the bottom in World Championship matches, but I kept my bulk shot fairly close to the hook. I had a couple of droppers that were almost on the bottom. It's a matter of holding back as hard as you can, but the World rules say you can't stop the bait totally. When you're hanging on to the rig, you don't see bites as well, so you have to keep it moving through steadily. Then the float pulls down a little bit, or does something out of the ordinary. I was helped that day because the bottom was very clean. I never caught up at all.

Within three or four minutes, I had caught my first dace. They were reasonable fish, 2 or 3 oz (56-85 g), and they were right on the bottom. I had to feed groundbait and maggot – a reasonable amount in small, hard balls – all the time because the feed was being swept away so quickly. If you didn't put in another ball a minute later, there was nothing left for the dace to come up to. I had to keep my own fish, and perhaps steal other people's. I've always tried to steal everybody else's fish! I got through a big container of groundbait, probably 5 or 6 lb (2.25-2.72 kg) of dry, and 2 pt (1 litre) of maggots, which is a lot to feed in groundbait. Those maggots must have been going down quite a long way, so they were drawing fish from other pegs as well.

It wasn't easy fishing. It was a horrible day, raining and windy, and I had a heavily overshotted rig that needed total concentration. But I felt comfortable. It was just like fishing in Ireland really: a ball of groundbait with maggots every cast, upstream of the float, and then running it down, holding it, running it down, holding it. Once you develop a rhythm, it becomes enjoyable.

Dick was with me when I caught my first fish. He made me net it but once he left, I started to swing them. I had

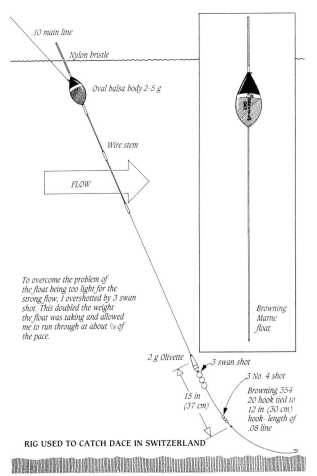

.10 main line

Nylon bristle

Oval balsa body 2-5 g

Wire stem

FLOW

To overcome the problem of the float being too light for the strong flow, I overshotted by 3 swan shot. This doubled the weight the float was taking and allowed me to run through at about ⅛ of the pace.

Browning Marne float

2 g Olivette — 3 swan shot

15 in (37 cm)

3 No. 4 shot

Browning 354 20 hook tied to 12 in (30 cm) hook- length of .08 line

RIG USED TO CATCH DACE IN SWITZERLAND

plenty of confidence in my tackle. I was using a size 18 hook with double maggot and 1½ lb (0.75 kg) line. You don't lose many dace on that. Fortunately, I didn't have to use a long pole. Twelve metres got you right to the other bank and I only needed 9 m.

I had a fair bit of line out. I wanted to run right down my peg, and I probably had 6 m to hand. I caught quite well. They came fairly steady right through the match and I was catching about 20 fish an hour. They died off a bit towards the end, but that's to be expected. The three hours flew by. I thought I had done well, because no one else was really catching much near me. I knew I was well up and I finished second in my section with between 60 and 70 fish, all dace, weighing 9 lb 4 oz 12 dr (4.217 kg). I caught more than half England's total weight and I was the only England team member to finish in the top four, which meant I was in the individual match the following day. Gerard Heulard of France won my section with 11 lb 15 oz (5.415 kg), but the French knew it was going to flow. They had big round floats, which were what was wanted.

It was a great first match for me. I had no tangles right the way through, and used the same rig all match. Whenever you are catching fish and you don't need to change your rig, you're pretty certain to be among the top places. Too many people make the mistake of trying different things, changing baits and tackle, even when they are catching. I was fortunate that I'd fished similar conditions in practice. It hadn't ever flowed as hard as it did this day, but I caught dace doing exactly the same thing as in practice.

After the match, it wasn't very clear what had happened, but it was obvious that we were in with a good chance of winning the team title. Kevin had caught late on. Tommy, drawn in a bad area, had struggled a bit, but Denis had done brilliantly from a poor area. Kevin, Ian and Denis were all fifth in their sections and Tommy was 11th. But you nearly always get a bad result, someone who is on not such a good peg. It happens in World Championships just as much as Nationals or ordinary team matches. It's no good moaning at that person, as I've heard some teams do. It happens to everyone, even the best in the world.

Anyway, we couldn't believe our bad luck when the result came through. We had the same number of points as Luxembourg – 28 – but they had pipped us on total weight by 20 lb 12 oz (9.412 kg) to 16 lb 9 oz 8 dr (7.258 kg). They had drawn end peg, which made a big difference on a water like that. One of the Luxembourg team foul-hooked a bream, and that was the difference between winning and losing. However, we soon realized how well we had done. It was the best-ever performance by an England team, and we had done it despite the misleading information that had been put out. We had adapted, and with a little more luck we would have won the match.

In those days, the individual match was fished on the following day, and in this case it was fished on a different river, the Broye at Salavaux. The previous few days' rain had turned the river, which was about the width of the Warwickshire Avon, into a raging torrent. I was the only England man fishing and I had the whole team behind me, giving me advice. It rained all day on the team match, it rained all that night and all the next day. I had never practised on this water, but it wouldn't have made any difference. I didn't have a bite. A few bream were caught on the end pegs and Bobby Smithers of Ireland, on peg 1, won it with 18 lb 12 oz (8.5 kg). But I wasn't too worried. The main thing was – and still is – the team event, and I can say that, even though I've won the individual twice.

Coming back to England was great. The phone never stopped ringing with congratulations. And it was great buying the angling papers that week!

THE ITALIAN JOB

That first match did wonders for my confidence, and the following year I was hopeful of making the squad again for Italy. After all, I won the World Club Team Championships there in 1983, and now I had started to believe that I really could hold my own in the England side.

The 1985 World Championships were held on the very same water where we had taken top weight in the World Club Team Championships, the River Arno in Florence, so it was probably going to be carp fishing, in which I had a lot of experience. In those days, there weren't waters everywhere full of carp, so I had some advantage with my experience on Layer pits. I knew how to make carp feed, and most importantly how to play them.

I was delighted when I got that telephone call from Dick. The Arno hadn't changed much. There was still plenty of carp, though there seemed to be more chub about. It was still very low, very clear, slow moving and immensely hot during the day. I caught a lot of fish, particularly carp, in practice, on all sorts of methods. Matches there draw big crowds, and there were a lot of Italians watching me.

We had worked out a variety of tactics, because the match was held in three sections. It was to be held on both sides of this very wide river, and there were a further three sections further downriver on a much deeper stretch that had been dredged out and was therefore

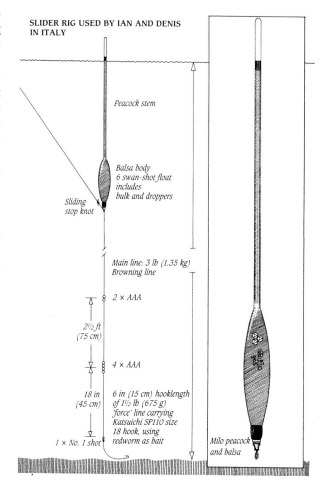

SLIDER RIG USED BY IAN AND DENIS IN ITALY

Peacock stem

Balsa body
6 swan-shot float includes bulk and droppers

Sliding stop knot

Main line: 3 lb (1.35 kg) Browning line

2 × AAA

2½ ft (75 cm)

4 × AAA

18 in (45 cm)

6 in (15 cm) hooklength of 1½ lb (675 g) 'force' line carrying Katsuichi SP110 size 18 hook, using redworm as bait

1 × No. 1 shot

Milo peacock and balsa

much slower moving. We had to work out a different tactic for each part. The section below the bridge was mainly catfish on worm fished with big sliders. That's where we really dominated because Denis, and particularly Ian, are masters with the slider. Kevin, who caught some chub up in the water, was also in the deep section. Tommy was on the bank where I had won the match two years previously, and I was on the opposite bank where it was going to be pole-fishing. We had caught a few carp in practice, but didn't catch any in the match. They were on the other side of the river, where they had the individual match the following day. Once again I made the team, with Dave Roper as reserve (though he was going to get his bit of glory the following day).

When I saw my peg, I just couldn't believe it. I've never had a peg before or since with so many fish in it. I had end peg by the bridge and it was solid with chub. They were just everywhere. When I cast, the surface erupted with fish weighing up to 2 lb (900 g). There seemed to be millions of them. The sun was on the water, so I could see them all. It looked like the sort of swim where you could catch 200 lb (90 kg) in three hours.

I was very excited, but my excitement was tempered a little because in practice we had spotted a lot of fish in the middle of the river, but when we chucked a waggler out we just couldn't get a bite from them. I knew I was not going to need two keepnets, but I still thought it was going to be good because I was on the end peg. However, I knew the top of my section, which could produce a lot of catfish and other fish, was very good as well.

I set up a couple of waggler rods, one for carp and a light waggler rod with just droppers, because it wasn't very deep, for chub. However, my main line of attack was going to be a very light pole rig, because we had found that to catch these chub, you had to fish light down the line with a

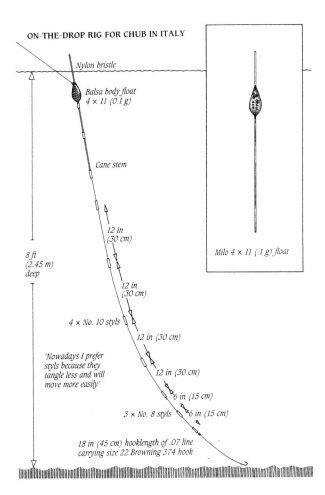

ON-THE-DROP RIG FOR CHUB IN ITALY

Nylon bristle

Balsa body float
4 × 11 (0.1 g)

Cane stem

12 in
(30 cm)

8 ft
(2.45 m)
deep

Milo 4 × 11 (.1 g) float

12 in
(30 cm)

4 × No. 10 styls

12 in (30 cm)

'Nowadays I prefer
styls because they
tangle less and will
move more easily'

12 in (30 cm)

6 in (15 cm)

3 × No. 8 styls   6 in (15 cm)

18 in (45 cm) hooklength of .07 line
carrying size 22 Browning 374 hook

very small float, feed, and flick the float out on top of the feed so that the hookbait was dropping through with the maggots.

There was a huge crowd, the largest I have ever seen for an angling match. I was lucky that I wasn't next to an Italian! I was really looking forward to the match; it looked like a dream peg with all these fish swimming around. Down to my left and through the bridge the water was full of chub as far as I could see. The water was black with them. But the float didn't disappear straight away, as I had expected. I started on the pole and it was 20 minutes before I caught a chub. After 90 minutes I was struggling. I had 10 fish, though they were all chub. Dick came down to me and he was panicking. They were catching well from the top end of my section, with some anglers having as much as 60 or 70 fish.

Dick was worried. He said, 'I want you to go out on worm and try and catch a better fish.' As it happened I wasn't doing that badly, but Dick didn't know that. Everyone else was catching catfish and Dick thought I was last in the section. So though these fish were still swimming around on the top, I went out with waggler and worm. In the last hour and a half, I didn't catch anything. In retrospect, I would have been better staying on those chub and winkling out an odd one here and there. If I had stayed with what I was doing, I would have picked up another half a dozen at least. To some extent, it was my fault for not informing Dick clearly enough what sort of weight I had, but I was still relatively inexperienced. It nearly cost us our first team title. Afterwards Dick said, 'If I'd left you alone, you'd have done better.'

My weight was 6 lb 4 oz 4 dr (2.537 kg), which put me 10th in my section. But there were some very big weights at the other end, so it was a really bad result for me. Looking back, I should have just carried on as I was, fishing out fine and long with the pole, feeding, and trying to make sure that the maggot dropped through with the feed. The fish I could see weren't feeding, and that's often the way. It's easy to be deceived by visible fish, only to waste a lot of time trying to catch them. I should have kept on for the ones that were feeding, the ones that were lower down and that I couldn't see.

It was such a frustrating match. To this day, I don't think I've ever been in a peg that had more fish in it. When I nearly broke the world record in Ireland in 1978, I don't think I had as many fish in my peg. This time, when I threw out my waggler, the whole surface erupted. It was full of fish. I was on millions of fish and couldn't catch them.

I felt terrible as I packed up. I knew I hadn't got that many fish and I was pleased in the end to come 10th. I was really worried I'd let the team down because everybody else had done so well. Tommy had won his section, so had Denis, while Kevin and Ian were second. As it happened, we won by one point from Italy. If it had been decided on weight, we would have finished second. We had 16 points and they had 17, but they had 44 lb 12 dr (19.979 kg) and we had 42 lb 9 oz 8 dr (19.320 kg). It was England's first win in the World Championships.

That was a memorable evening. We'd won in Italy, the home of match angling and, with France, the strongest angling nation. From that moment on, we had joined the best in the world, and ever since we have been the team to beat. The Italians were very good about it. They are so sociable. I still remember that year: working all day then strolling out in the evenings, eating wonderful food and sitting outside a café drinking and talking about fishing.

In those days, every team had one free place for the individual championship, along with anyone who had finished in the top four. So all the others were fishing except me. Dave Roper, who was reserve along with Alan McAtee, got his chance to fish and he won it with 14 lb 1 oz 4 dr (6.405 kg) of carp. The banquet that night was very emotional, especially .when they called us up to collect our trophies. And it was great coming back to England. I love reading about the team's achievements, and thinking, 'Is that really me there?' The press have always been extremely good to me.

Even though I had a bad result, I never really worried about whether it might affect my place. I did nothing wrong, merely tried another tactic under Dick's instruction. He tried to advise me as he saw it, and thought I had to force my way up the section. But this is what a manager is for. He has to make things happen and use his judgment. Teams that appoint managers or team captains have to accept that the boss can get things wrong as well as right. When I won it in Hungary, Dick's influence was to make all the difference.

CAUGHT SHORT IN FRANCE

My memories of Strasbourg in 1986 are none too happy, though before the match I was brimming with confidence. I went to the water, the Alsace Canal, a couple of times with Dick and we spent a lot of time there. The water looked tailor-made for me, though it was a peculiar venue for the French to choose. Even their team didn't think they had a chance. It looked as if they had chosen it because there were plenty of hotels nearby.

I caught a lot of fish in practice. The water was just like Switzerland, but it was a much bigger river, needing floats of 8-10 g. Once again, it needed a ball of groundbait every cast. We mixed stones into the groundbait to make it sink faster. This was easy because there was a load of gravel on the bank. I caught a lot of good fish including barbel and bream in practice and I was really looking forward to match day. For the first time, I felt really confident that I would make the team, because I'd caught a lot of fish in practice and I knew how to catch them.

It meant size 18 or 20 hooks to 1½ lb (0.75 kg) bottoms. We used round-bodied floats of up to 10 g with quite a bit of line to the pole so we could run down our pegs. It was all pole fishing: there was nothing else we could do because it flowed so hard. The only exception was one particular bit that went backwards. It was a sort of back eddy for six or seven pegs, horrible because you

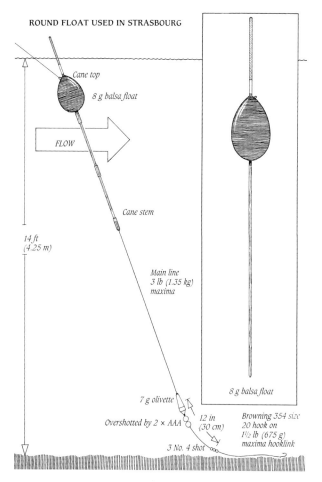

ROUND FLOAT USED IN STRASBOURG

Cane top

8 g balsa float

FLOW

Cane stem

14 ft
(4.25 m)

Main line
3 lb (1.35 kg)
maxima

7 g olivette

Overshotted by 2 × AAA

12 in
(30 cm)

3 No. 4 shot

8 g balsa float

Browning 354 size
20 hook on
1½ lb (675 g)
maxima hooklink

couldn't get out to the flow. And that's where I drew. With the poles I've got now, I could have got across and I would have done all right, fishing at 17 or 18 m. Then, my longest pole was 14 m and I could hardly hold it at that. I couldn't get out into the flow so I had to fish in the slack water, which is the last place I wanted to fish. Food is carried in the flow on a big river like that, and the fish become accustomed to the pace of the water.

The team still kid me about the look on my face when I realized where I had drawn. I had a face like thunder, I'm told. They reckon I went to the peg with the wrong attitude. But being on a river that I loved to fish, and on which I had always caught fish in the flow, it was a huge disappointment to find I would not have a chance. But I'll admit that maybe I should not have shown my disappointment so openly! I'm not usually very emotional, but that day I really let my feelings out.

When I got to the peg, I decided that I had to fish the slack water as far out as I could. It was a terribly difficult match because I just didn't know where to throw my feed. One minute it was pulling hard to the left, next minute it had stopped. I couldn't figure out what was happening with my feed. I fished a 2.5 g float and fed a lot lighter than I would have done in the flow, putting in some bloodworm and joker, but mainly pinkies and maggot. I caught a little skimmer after about 20 minutes, then a bigger bream and two or three little fish. I weighed in 1 lb 15 oz (879 g), which gave me eighth in the section.

It was all so frustrating because I knew that if I could have got out into the flow, I would have caught well. Maybe I would have had to wait two, even two-and-a-half hours, but I would have taken a couple of big fish. I just knew that with perseverance and accurate feeding, I could catch and beat most other people.

Looking back, I suppose it was a pretty good performance from a bad peg, but it was one of those days when everything went wrong for us as a team. Tommy was fifth in his section and Kevin second, but Ian was 12th and Denis, of all people, had a blank. You would normally back Denis to catch every time. There were very few little fish to catch, and it was either catch in the flow or nothing. In addition, Ian was well down in his section. As a team, we finished seventh, which for us was an absolute disaster. Dick spent most of the day with Denis trying to catch a fish. Once you're catching and you're half-right, he leaves you alone. You know when you're doing well, because you never see him. So when he's sitting beside you, you think, 'Oh no, something's going wrong.'

Just to compound a bad year, the individual match was fished on a featureless canal, the Canal du Marne au Rhin, behind the European Community building. We had three men in the final but none did any good. The fish were at either end of the venue and if you were in the middle, you hadn't got a chance. Hans Wever of Holland won the individual with 8 lb 11 oz (3.935 kg) and the best we did was Kevin, who came eighth with 2 lb 12 oz (1.247 kg).

As a team, we never really had an inquest about what went wrong, though. If Denis had caught, we would have been right up there. We had a bad draw, but the Italians did it a little better than us by feeding a lot more pinkies than we did. It just seemed to attract more fish.

RUNNING THE BANK IN PORTUGAL

I was back in the squad for Portugal, but I didn't fish in the team match that year. I was very close to getting in, but if anyone deserved to be dropped, it was me. In practice I fished a bit too far out and did one or two things that weren't right. It was waggler fishing pure and simple, and we had a squad of brilliant waggler anglers, including Steve Gardener for the first time. Someone once said: 'When Steve gets in that team, you'll never get him out.' It looks as if they were right! And Kevin, Denis, Tommy and Ian are all very strong on the waggler.

The match, on the River Mondego at Coimbra, involved a fairly long cast and feeding with sticky maggots. The target fish were small barbel, 2 lb (0.90 kg) being a very big fish. They'd come up in the water, feeding on the drop. They weren't that hard to catch, you just had to be efficient at catching them.

This was the first World Championships where sticky maggot had been used. We'd practised with it in Italy but didn't use it in the end. We had discovered that these barbel preferred loosefeed to groundbait, but there was no way you could loosefeed at a distance – especially as the match was fished in a hurricane!

When sticky maggot was first used in England, anglers used Horlicks. Now special powder is available. I always use the Italian brands, because you don't need to use as much powder, and they seem to attract fish better than the English brands. Sieve the maggots to remove all sawdust or maize, then put them in a large, very shallow tray or groundbait bowl. Add just a small amount of powder, then damp the maggots either with drops of water or by using a fine-mist spray. You only need a little water to make the maggots bind. If they dry out, add just a little more water. Cover them if it is raining or you will have maggots everywhere! If you want a hard ball of sticky maggot, put a little maize on your hands.

This was the first year that I hadn't fished. Although watching top anglers is a very good way for a matchman to improve, I didn't learn much that day. I was more worried about how we were doing. Dick was running one half of the match, I was running the other, and we were meeting in the middle, chatting and going back. I don't like running, but I think just to be part of the squad is fantastic so I didn't worry about it too much. Somebody had to be left out and in my heart, I felt it was fair that it was me. It was an easy match for us. We had such a good side for that sort of fishing and we were easy winners. We had just nine points, well clear of Italy with 18 and Austria with 33. Our lowest position was Steve, third in section. Kevin and Denis won their sections, while Ian and Tommy were second.

I fished in the individual match the following day and drew next to Ian, beating him by a few grammes. I had 2 lb (900 g) and Ian weighed in 1 lb 10 oz (735 g). We had to throw right across the river to get a bite. The previous day, England had done so well that the whole team fished the individual match, though Clive Branson of Wales took the title with 5 lb 8 oz (2.5 kg). He did it by being aware that he needed a few more fish, scaling up and bringing them in a bit faster than Kevin, who was next to him and came second with 5 lb 7 oz 12 dr (2.485 kg). Denis was third to round off a great year for us. Clive, who had been individual runner-up in Strasbourg the previous year, is like Kevin and Roberto Trabucco of Italy, a very good, natural angler. He's the best angler to come out of Wales.

Even when you haven't actually fished in the team match, the spirit is such that you still feel you have contributed towards the success. And I shall never forget the after-match banquet, when the England team walked into the hall. We were the last team in, and it all went deadly silent. Then everybody stood up and clapped us. It was a wonderful feeling.

BELGIUM, AND MY FIRST SECTION WIN

Dick showed that even the best anglers have to win their places when he named the squad for the Van Damme Canal in Belgium and his two favourites, Denis and Tommy, were not in. It looked like being a pole and bloodworm match, so he brought in Vinny Smith, Dave Vincent and Dave Roper. Steve Gardener had made a point of fishing a lot of bloodworm matches, and I suppose my pole experience won me a place. I had a lot of experience fishing with bloodworm.

This match turned on its head all you read about a water being easier in practice than it is on the day. In practice it was absolutely diabolical. We had a job to get a bite sometimes. There didn't seem to be any fish. In practice, it was the hardest water I have ever fished on a world match. There were some tiny ruffe to be caught close in with 2 m whips. Then there were odd perch, roach, skimmer bream, a few carp and a very attractive fish called a vimba. Because it was an easy run to Belgium, I had gone over with Steve and Dave Vincent beforehand to learn more about the canal.

Our practice sessions soon showed that it was a bloodworm and joker water. There were hardly any fish to catch in practice, which is always a sign that things will be very hard. We were sometimes getting only 1 lb (450 g) of fish, and sometimes we couldn't get a bite for two hours. When it came to the official practice, things were no better. We had to fish off the match length because it was closed, but there just weren't many fish around.

Practice sessions taught us that the fish didn't like too much groundbait, but Dave Vincent discovered that feeding joker with just a little bit of grey leam to bind it was much better than feeding groundbait. This was to be our secret weapon on the day, especially as the Continentals were expected to put in their usual barrage of groundbait. We had a big argument over whether to put in groundbait on the pole line. I was adamant that we had to feed this line, even though only one or two of us would probably catch on it. As it happened, it worked well for Steve on both days. But if a method only works for one person, it's a bonus.

So there were three lines to consider: under your feet for the little pope, a pole line on 11-12 m for skimmers and the far bank with a waggler for vimba, roach and skimmers again. On the far line we fished it light: 22 hooks to 1 lb (0.5 kg) line, with the aim of catching on the drop. This was the first year of the two-day championship, with the individual title settled by the angler who had the best performances over both days. It is a much fairer system.

We were expecting a real struggle, but it didn't turn out like that at all. When we got to our pegs, fish were topping everywhere. I couldn't believe it. Nobody had been allowed to fish for them and I suppose they had become less cautious. I also suspect that the Belgians put in some more fish.

I started fishing with a 2 m whip for these little ruffe and caught a couple, but then I saw the angler on my left catch a fish across on waggler. I thought: 'I've got to go straight

It's no surprise that my face looks grim; none of us was prepared for the Van Damme Canal to produce so well. I was expecting to struggle for a few little pope but the float kept going under with proper fish!

over there.' In practice I'd never thrown out a waggler that had gone under straight away, but this time it disappeared immediately and I had a lovely roach. Out again, another lovely roach. It was just easy. It was the easiest match I've ever fished in my life. Within 20 minutes, I must have been winning the section by miles. I don't know what weight I had then, but I was catching a fish every cast.

Of course, they didn't keep coming like that, and I finished catching odd skimmers on the drop using two bloodworms. I fished waggler all day, finished with 5 lb 10 oz 4 dr (2.558 kg) and won my section easily.

Those vimba were the key fish. They're very colourful – red fins and golden underneath – and streamlined like a barbel. Some were over 1 lb (450 g), and they weren't too cautious either. I didn't get any that big; most of my catch was skimmers and roach, but I had plenty of fish.

Elsewhere Dave Roper won his section on the waggler and Steve did well on the pole, finishing second. Kevin was fourth. But there were a couple of sections where it was tough, and Vinnie Smith just couldn't get the bonus waggler

fish. I remember him saying afterwards: 'I must have killed a robin'. Things didn't go well for him the next day either. The tiny pope that were our bankers just weren't in his swim in quantity – and he's a brilliant bloodworm angler.

On the next day, we didn't change things around very much. Most of us had got it right. We expected that we would have to work a bit harder on the small ruffe and we talked a lot about them, because we realized they were important in areas where there weren't any larger fish. The rest of our feeding tactics were clearly correct. We'd been surprised by all those bigger fish, but the quality of the team had shown in the speed with which we adjusted. We were still a bit sceptical about whether the quality fish would show again. Our closest rivals were the Italians. We had beaten them on the big fish sections, but they were way in front of us on the small fish sections. And that's how the pattern went both days.

I drew a reasonably good area again, and fed it exactly the same but started off straight on the waggler. I caught early on and was getting roach and skimmers steadily. It

Left: Another quality roach comes my way during the 1988 championships in Belgium.

Above: If there were fish in your peg, then the heavy feeding approach could pay off, as Steve Gardener proved in Bulgaria, 1989.

We just took the team event on weight from Italy. Both teams had 50 points, but we totalled 42 lb 6 oz 12 dr (19.242 kg) and they had 31 lb 9 oz 4 dr (14.324 kg). Those big fish had proved a real bonus for us. It looked as if we might even get the individual, but Jean-Pierre Fougeat of France took that. Dave was third in his section after having the highest weight on the first day. Steve was runner-up overall, having won his section on the second day. Kevin drew a tough area and was ninth in his section (a bad result by his standards!), and Vinnie struggled again but managed eighth.

I felt I had fished really well. But just to show that one should never get too confident, I had my worst-ever result the next year in Bulgaria, when I got it completely wrong.

THE ATTACK THAT FAILED

The Bulgarian match water was a rowing course at Plovdiv that had just been built. It was 7-8 ft (2.15-2.45 m) deep, dead straight, with a sloping concrete bank to sit on. I did best during practice, and caught loads of fish. There were plenty of fish in the water: carp, bleak, bream, and a strange bottom-feeding fish with a wedge-shaped mouth.

During practice we fed heavily with maggot, and carp would move in. They hadn't been caught before so they'd take massive hooks. I put on some Irish gear, 5 lb (2.25 kg) Maxima, a Model Perfect 10, with four or five maggots and 4 lb (2 kg) hook length. No flick tip, just an 11 m pole, and I'd have a 4 lb (1.8 kg) carp in the net in about 10 seconds. This rig also brought other fish that we could swing in. But it was all too good, and it was easy to get carried away. We should have been warned by the 1976 championships in Bulgaria, when nobody was allowed on the match length and it fished totally differently to the practice stretch. On this occasion, too, we couldn't go anywhere near the match length.

We thought it would roughly be the same, but it wasn't. It was harder, but we were still expecting pretty good fishing. My experience of carp fishing is that if you feed enough, they'll move in. That was my mistake.

The team was Steve, Denis, Tommy, Kevin and myself, with Alan McAtee as reserve. We were pretty confident that we would do well. To some extent, we took into account that it could be less productive by deciding on waggler fishing with little balls of groundbait if it was hard, and with pole or waggler closer in when those carp and whatever else came along.

I was so confident that I started on the pole. Nothing came along, but I'd fed out on the waggler line. I was

was obvious from the outset that it wasn't quite as good as the day before. I had to chop and change to keep the fish coming: moving on to the pole line to see if I could catch something, then coming just off the far shelf. By this stage, I was fishing very fine with bloodworm and things were going well until, after two hours, I hooked an enormous carp. It ran downstream for five pegs. It must have been a good 15 lb (6.8 kg). It certainly didn't do me any favours because it absolutely ruined my peg.

I finished fifth in my section with 1 lb 6 oz 12 dr (645 g). Looking back, I don't think there was much else I could have done to boost my weight, except perhaps to concentrate on coming off the far shelf a bit more. I caught a couple of roach later in the competition towards the middle on waggler, but we had never caught there before. I'd just done it in desperation.

convinced I was going to catch carp. I had to go out on the waggler after about 20 minutes, but kept piling in ground-bait and maggot on the nearside. After 30 minutes, I caught a couple of these bottom-feeders of about 10 oz (285 g). But that was about it. At the other end of my section, they were catching one or two small fish and the occasional carp too. Piling in the bait didn't work after all. There were eight carp caught in my section, all 3-4 lb (1.35-1.8 kg) and I ended up with four fish for 1 lb 13 oz (882 g). It put me 19th in my section, the worst I had ever done by far. Steve, who's from the same mould as me when carp are around, did disastrously as well. He was 14th with 6lb 10 oz (2.551 kg).

Fortunately Tommy and Denis fished it sensibly. Tommy won his section with 20 lb 14 oz 8 dr (9.483 kg) and Kevin was third with 8 lb 11 oz 4 dr (3.942 kg), while Denis was ninth in his with 17 lb 8 dr (7.726 kg), so we were still in with a shout. But I didn't learn. I went back and did the same thing the next day. I can't believe now that I was so stupid, but I was so convinced that heavy feeding would draw the carp, I was blinkered because we had caught so many fish in practice doing it that way that I just thought I had a bad section. Looking back, it's obvious that I should never have attacked it as I did. If I fished it again now, I'd feed carefully with tiny balls of groundbait as far as I could throw. If I had done this at the time then I would probably have had a good weight. I think that's why Tommy did so well that year. He took it very cautiously and as a result, fished it right.

I only learnt near the end of the second day, when I went out further and fed smaller balls of groundbait. I picked up two or three fish in the last hour. I had a better weight, 3 lb 2 oz 8 dr (1.432 kg), but one end of my section fished brilliantly for 10 or 11 pegs. I was 21st in my section. It was an absolute disaster. To make it worse, the rest of the team had done well. Tommy was second with 13 lb 2 oz 8 dr (5.971 kg), so was Steve with 21 lb 6 oz 4 dr (9.703 kg), Kevin was fifth with 16 lb 6 oz 8 dr (7.442 kg) and Denis sixth with 3 lb 9 oz (1.616 kg). Our team totalled 83 points and nearly half of them came from me because I hadn't used my brain.

Luckily Steve had drawn on a load of fish and had caught bream. If you were on fish, it was like that. You didn't need to feed, but where there weren't fish, you were best putting hardly anything in. We finished third behind Wales, who won it easily with 48 points, and Italy with 68. But at least Tommy had won the individual title. It couldn't happen to a nicer chap.

ON TOP OF THE WORLD
I would not have been surprised if Dick had dropped me after that. But he never said anything. I think I kept my place for the River Drava at Maribor in Yugoslavia the next year because he knew I'd attacked it. I don't think I fished badly. I just fed it wrong, but it was so easy to do after what had happened in practice. Sometimes you need to be aggressive in fishing.

Now I can see where I went wrong. Where everyone practised, all the feed had gone in and there were loads of eager fish. Then we fished a match where the fish had never even seen a maggot. Thank goodness Dick didn't hold it against me, because the following year, 1990, was my first individual win.

The squad was exactly the same as Bulgaria, but with Mark Downes instead of Alan McAtee. Dick had been out there and realized it was a pole job. It flowed very hard and because it was about 18 ft (5.5 m) deep, running line was out of the question. It was a perfect water for me, bringing back memories of Strasbourg: big floats overshotted, running down the peg, with a ball of groundbait every cast. The bad news, we were to discover, was that there were very few fish.

The main fish were like an oversized gudgeon. We called them 'cigars', because that's just what they looked like, though they were actually barbel-gudgeon, a fish unique to Yugoslavia. They were about 3 oz (85 g) each: long, fat, bottom-feeding fish that wanted a bait crept along the bottom. There were a few in every peg. They were the ones that you had to catch. To give you an idea of how hard it was, we thought we would be lucky if we all caught a fish. You were looking for two or three fish for good points. The best weight we had in about 20 practice sessions was 6 lb (2.70 kg). There were also a few roach and big bream, 3 lb (1.35 kg) fish. Bait was double blood-worm on a 20 hook with reasonably fine elastic, but not too fine, because with a 10 g float, you need to make sure that you set the hook when you strike.

We quickly discovered that the only way to catch was using a pole as long as possible. I ended up fishing with 17 m (I could have done with a pole like that in Strasbourg) and it got me a couple of bonus fish. I started on 14 m and worked out from there. We knew we had the tactics right because every other team was copying us.

I was confident I'd get in the team. Kevin and I both had a lot of experience at this method, from fishing the Bann in Northern Ireland in flood and putting floats up to 19 g through it. This was going to be very different from the

Another net fish and Tommy is on his way to becoming world champion in Bulgaria.

Bann, however. We were looking for six bites if everything went according to plan.

With such large, overshotted floats, the bites were very difficult to see because of the powerful water and small fish. They usually consisted of a tremble on the float. You had to put the float down so the antenna was just above the top, and so you could see any little deviation. Running an overshotted float through perfectly is hard enough, but at 14 m and longer it's very difficult indeed, especially when feeding has to be done so accurately as well. It's probably the hardest method of all to master.

The groundbait mix was very stiff, with joker in it and some pinkies – not too many, though, because it makes the groundbait break up too easily. Hookbait was sometimes double bloodworm and a pinkie, sometimes three bloodworm, creeping slowly along the bottom. Denis was named as reserve. Imagine having a team so good that you can leave out Denis White!

I drew a fairly even section on the first day, and within 15 minutes I had caught a 'cigar' and netted it. Once I'd caught that one fish, I just had to keep running through, hoping to catch a big bream. I started at 14 m and caught four fish, but after an hour I couldn't get another bite so I went up to 15.5 m. In that next hour I caught two more fish and then it died, so I went to 17 m and caught one more. That last one didn't really matter. The second weight in my section was one roach of 14 oz (395 g). It was diabolical fishing. There were 24 blanks on the first day and 21 on the second. The Frenchman below me had one fish, the lad on the right never caught. I finished up with seven 'cigars' for 1 lb 15 oz 4 dr (886 g), and won my section easily.

The team had not done so well, largely because Tommy, the World Champion, hadn't caught a fish. It was a disastrous year for him because he didn't get a bite the next day either. Fishing can be very cruel sometimes.

There was nothing much to say after the first day, though we spent some time talking about tiny fish that could be caught right in the edge. One of these might avoid a dry net. They were in odd pegs and you could

The bream was a bonus, but I still had a fine net of roach and small perch.

catch them, so our instructions the next day were to go for a little fish from the off just to see if they were around. I did it for about a minute but didn't catch one. However, I had a feeling it wouldn't matter, because I had drawn a lovely peg, even though the Dutchman who was there the previous day had caught nothing.

It was E24, the end of the match length, and I knew it was good. It was only about 12 ft (4 m) deep (shallow compared to the rest of the stretch), dead level and it flowed far less hard than much of the venue. You could fish it with a 3 g float. When I knew where I was going, I was rubbing my hands together, because my section got progressively worse as the numbers got lower.

I had a fantastic match. Within a minute I'd thrown the little pole up the bank because I knew what was out there. I was fishing about 4 g, once again slightly overshotted and just running through. About the third run down, I had a bite and got a little roach. Then I got another, and from then on I had an abundance of fish. I finished with 4 lb 8 oz 8 dr (2.055 kg), including a bream of more than 2 lb (900 g). I won my section by more than 3 lb (1.35 kg). It was lovely, easy fishing. I fished at 14 m all day, and though the swim died towards the end I just knew it was my day. I fed it right, fed it accurately and no-one else was catching.

About halfway through, when I netted the bream, it suddenly occurred to me that I could become World Champion. Though I lost another bream, I started to think; 'Who else won their section yesterday?' But Dick came along and he had worked it out. I felt just great inside. And though afterwards I was full of happiness that I won it, I was unhappy for Tommy, who had blanked twice. He must have felt dreadful, especially after winning the title the year before.

We finished runner-up team, tying with Italy on 89 points but beating them easily on weight. France won it with 60 points. But if Tommy had managed to get even a tiny fish both days, we would have won again. We had some consolation because Kevin was individual runner-up.

I can't remember much about that night. It was another of those very emotional times. Kevin and I had both phoned home, so we were late walking into the dining hall. As we came in, everyone stopped talking, stood up and clapped us. I don't think I took in the trophies, the photographs and all the other things that come with being World Champion. It's something that you strive for all your life, but you never really believe it will happen because the chances of becoming World Champion are so remote. Even when I was first picked to fish for England, I never

Back to school: we try on our England caps before the 1991 World Championships in Hungary.

even considered that one day I would be World Champion. My dream then was to be part of the team that wins the title.

Thinking back, it was the first day, not the second, that really won me the title. I caught seven fish from a bad area. It doesn't sound a lot, but many in my section didn't have a bite. My confidence was so high that I would have felt confident of catching some fish in most places.

My return to England was tremendous. I got home quite late at night, but Peter Clapperton, Billy Hughes and some friends were waiting up for me with champagne. The phone didn't stop ringing that week. Many people offered congratulations, and people made other offers too, of tie-ups on various things. I was unable to accept most of them because of my tie-up with Browning, but it was great just to be asked. Suddenly, I was a hot property!

DOUBLE TOP

Of course, winning the World Championship is the peak of any match fisherman's achievement. I never thought that lightning could strike twice and give me the title again, let alone in successive years, but when we saw the 1991 venue in Hungary, we knew we were going to catch a lot of fish. It was the opposite of Yugoslavia. Our main problem was that it was so good, we had to sort out the fastest method to catch the fish.

The water at Szeged was a rowing course, exactly the same as Holme Pierrepont at Nottingham, and it was the best world match venue I've ever fished. It was a still water with a little bit of tow on it, about 7-8 ft (2.15-2.45 m) deep, and fishing was with a whip or long pole and short line. Everybody had exactly the same depth. You could move along from one peg to the next the following day,

Right: Tommy Pickering gets mixing before the start of the 1991 Championships.

Left: The rowing course at Szeged: featureless on top, but it was full of fish and brought me my second world title.

plummet up and it was exactly the same. You didn't have to move anything. The only thing that altered slightly was your close-in line. To make it even better, there was a reasonable head of fish all the way through. It was just the sort of water I like, because I could attack it.

In practice, Dick counted 23 different species of fish. There were all sorts: carp, a lot of roach, sturgeon, grass carp, big bleak, funny fish that looked like chub but fed like dace right on the top, but mainly there were lots and lots of little perch close in. We were catching 15-16 lb (6.8-7.25 kg) of them in practice, and sometimes up to 30 lb (13.6 kg) of roach in three hours. It was terrific fishing. The main baits were maggot and caster. We didn't bother about bloodworm because we were pestered by these little perch and we could catch them much faster on maggot.

We weren't certain of the best tactics even on the morning of the match. It was easy to get carried away doing the wrong thing. We were catching perch at three a minute in practice, so we cut down the tips on our poles in order to haul out fish faster.

Come match day, it can be a very different story. It's all right when six of you in a line are feeding, but all the feed going in on the day can make the fish behave very differently. You go in with a maggot, expecting the float to go straight under, and it just stays still. The expectation of those perch feeding nearly cost me the World Championship, but I changed tactics just in time.

I drew peg E25, two or three off the end peg. I expected plenty of perch. In the pre-baiting period, I put two little balls with bloodworm and joker on a 2 m line and a dozen jaffas on 12 metres with joker and a few casters in it. The plan was to keep feeding balls of groundbait on this line to bring the fish in while I was catching perch. Then I put out six more balls on about 20 metres in case I had to go out on the waggler. I was all set for the usual rush of perch, but it was far harder than I expected.

I couldn't get a bite on maggot so I put on bloodworm and started to catch odd fish, but certainly not fast enough. I was getting worried. After about 45 minutes I had 40 perch, which wasn't very good because Dick came down and said there was a Frenchman who had 70-odd. It was because I was fishing too heavy. We had all started on the short pole with a stiff flick tip and a 20 hook to about 0.10 mm line. Our floats were too big as well. We were using about 0.5 g and we should have been using 0.2 g, fishing with size 22s, a single bloodworm and fine flick tips.

I knew it didn't feel right. I don't know why, but I started to lay off the groundbait and just loosefeed casters on the

far line while still fishing for the perch. Loosefed casters was not part of the team plan at all. In fact, it was quite contrary to what we had worked out, but I just had a sixth sense that it was the right thing to do. If I'd kept feeding groundbait I don't think I would have caught as well.

We were planning to fish for perch for an hour, but Dick came down and said: 'I'd go out now if I were you.' This made me switch to the long pole earlier than I had intended to. Without that advice, I wouldn't have been World Champion again.

As soon as I went out, the float went straight under and I got a roach of about 3½ oz (100 g). From then on, every time I went out, the float went under. It was dream fishing. They were mainly roach, but I had a few big bleak, some of those surface-feeding dace-like fish, and two grass carp of about 1 lb (450 g) each. Unlike most carp, which roar off, grass carp just swim round in circles. I alternated between caster and maggot. I couldn't work out which was better so I was putting three pouches of caster to one pouch of maggot. I finished the day with 13 lb 11 oz 4 dr (6.219 kg), won my section easily and had the highest weight in the match. It could have been even more, but I lost a carp of about 6 lb (2.7 kg).

Kevin had done the same as me – changing from groundbait to loosefeed – and won his section with just under 13 lb 10 oz 4 dr (6.290 kg). We were leading on the first day, with Steve and Denis finishing fifth with 5 lb 10 oz 12 dr (2.572 kg) and 4 lb 7 oz 4 dr (2.019 kg), but Tommy and Denis drawing in a harder section, coming 11th with 3 lb 2 oz (1.417 kg).

It's funny looking back on that day. There were two things that made all the difference: Dick telling me to go out on the long pole, and loosefeeding rather than putting in groundbait. I still don't know why I did it. I'd always caught on groundbait in practice. Perhaps that sixth sense warned me that if it was harder for the perch, it was going to be harder for the roach and other fish, too.

We talked it through for the following day and decided that the perch were far more important than we had anticipated. In some places we might have to fish a long pole and a short line and be happy to catch perch – which is what Denis did. I knew my gear was too heavy, so I was up until about 1 am completely changing to fine rigs. I recall

Fish of this size are a a real bonus in a world match; Kevin holds tight as he puts it into the net.

saying to Kevin, who was sharing a room with me then: 'These perch can make a difference between whether you're World Champion or not.' But Kevin didn't change his rigs. It cost him the world title.

On the next day I drew peg D2 in the middle of the match length. I knew it was going to be much harder. I had decided to loosefeed rather than use groundbait, but for some reason I concentrated on maggot rather than caster, which had caught me a load of fish the day before. I had an Italian on my right and Bobby Smithers of Ireland on my left, so I had two tough anglers who could not let me get away with much.

I started on the inside again, but with very light gear. It made all the difference. I had about 80 or 90 fish in the first hour and was winning the section. They were about 30 to the pound, so I probably had 3 lb (1.35 kg) – a good start. Even so, I disciplined myself to keep loosefeeding with maggot. It meant I was not catching the perch quite as fast, but it was vital for what came later.

The perch were still coming strong after an hour. I said to Bobby Smithers, 'Go and see if any roach are out there yet.' He had about 40 perch and was way behind me, but as soon as he went out, he caught a roach. That was enough for me. I put my little pole down, went out and it was just like the day before.

I think the key lay in loosefed maggots, although use of a much lighter float was also a factor. I know they were fishing heavier on either side. I was using light line and fishing on the drop for these fish, right from the top to the bottom. Between the second and third hour they were coming really strongly, and though the peg died a bit, I was still catching odd perch and roach. I also had one grass carp, and finished with 11 lb 4 dr (4.997 kg). I could have had even more, except I again lost a carp of about 7 lb (3.15 kg). The Frenchman in my section had about 300 little perch and weighed in about 9 lb (4.15 kg) for second place.

I had no idea I was on line to win the individual title again. I heard Kevin was about 10th in his section, but then he had caught a carp of about 5 lb (2.25 kg). I was delighted, because it then looked certain that he had won his section. I didn't mind coming second to him! I knew I'd got a reasonable weight, but I thought he was bound to have more than 11 lb (5 kg). As it happened, his total over the two days was just short of mine. We both had two section wins and got two points, but I had 24 lb 13 oz 4 dr (10.995 kg), and he had 24 lb 7 oz 4 dr (11.091 kg). I had become only the second person to win the title in succes-

sive years. The other was Robert Tesse in 1959 and 1960, but that was in the days when there were only eight teams taking part in the match.

We won by four points from France, 44 to 48, with Italy third on 51. On the rostrum there was Kevin, myself, and my other best friend, Jan van Schendel of Holland. I couldn't have asked for more.

Kevin had won his section with 10 lb 12 oz 4 dr (4.883 kg), and although the others didn't do quite as well, we had done more than enough to win the team event too. Tommy was seventh with 7 lb 12 dr (1.096 kg) in his section, Steve was seventh as well with 13 lb 12 oz 12 dr (6.261 kg) and Denis was 10th with 4 lb 3 oz (1.899 kg).

Looking back, that was the best venue I've ever fished because there were just so many fish. The weights may not have been brilliant, but by World Championship standards, when you get all that feed going in and all that noise, it was a superb result. I wish it could be like that every year!

The post-match banquet was held on a restaurant boat and that was quite a night because it was my stag night, too. Just a couple of days later, I got married to Bernadette. What with the celebrations for the team, the celebrations for me winning the individual again and my stag night as well, it was a very drunken night indeed. One of the few things I can remember about it was being bundled into a taxi, but not much else. I had my trophies when I woke up so somebody must have looked after me!

There was no champagne for me that year when I got home – though there was something even better. Peter was so delighted that he bought me my own personalised Mercedes. And five days later, I got married. That was quite a memorable week!

First and second in Hungary: Kevin and I as smart as you'll ever see us.

Milo Columbo, a generous man and a great angler. He makes some of the best floats in the world.

AN IRISH NIGHTMARE

In most circumstances, I would have been rubbing my hands at the prospect of defending my title on the River Erne in Northern Ireland. I know half the fish by name there! But I had never fished the Belleek section, which was usually used by game fishermen. I'm told it was coarse-fished in 1976 on the Benson & Hedges Championship, but was so bad that it was never used again. It's not hard to see why. I just don't know why the Irish chose it. We went out to practise and didn't catch at all well. To make it worse, there were two weeks of heavy rain leading up to the match.

The match was a nightmare. It produced the worst-ever result in the World Championships, with about half the anglers failing to catch a fish on both days. And there was so little skill about it. You just needed to be able to fish a big slider, though the Italians did well on the Bolognese method (see pages 142-144).

We had been over there many times and found out how to catch. In fact, it fished quite well for a home international, when waggler and groundbait worked, but that was at a different time of year and there was no flow. On the match day, because of all the rain, the Irish tried to run off some of the water, so it was running hard at night and steady during the day. This unsettled the fish even more.

There was a squad of 10 for this match with some excellent waggler anglers such as Dave Harrell and Keith Hobson. I was pleased to be picked, even though I had become one of the senior members of the squad. Dick knew it was a difficult water. I think he made a wise choice not to bring in new anglers, because to have a dry net on your first World Championship can have a huge effect on your confidence.

By the time the match came round, we knew there would be loads of blanks. Bets were being placed on how many blanks there would be. The draw was crucial – and my draw was terrible on the first day. I just didn't stand a chance of defending my title. I knew my section was going to be tough, but I had no idea it was going to be as bad as it was. In practice, we had always caught perch between 12 dr (21 g) and 3 oz (85 g). We thought one or two were guaranteed, but they didn't show at all.

I drew A18, and the match is one of the least memorable I have ever fished. I didn't catch anything, or even have a bite. It was just a matter of running a slider through, a third of the way out, and hoping. During practice we found that it would very occasionally go under, and there would be a bream on the end.

We didn't even need to fish it light. I used 16s and 14s with a couple of maggots, or worm and maggot. There was no point in putting on a 22. The roach and perch were just as likely to have it on the big hook, but nothing took. I didn't have a bite and recorded my first dry net in the World Championships. I was in the middle of 11 blanks. I don't think there's ever been a section like it in World Championships for lack of fish. Tommy drew in that section the next day and blanked again.

I suppose that before the match it was at the back of my mind that I could make history and win the World Championships three times in a row, but I never had a chance, or even half a chance to do so. I don't feel I let the team down. There was nothing I could have done.

It was tough when television crews and the rest of the press asked me how I felt at the end of the match. But part of my responsibility as World Champion was to face up to people in situations like that. It wasn't easy because I felt so disappointed. It even crossed my mind that Dick might drop me for the second day and fish Mark Downes. I was the only one who had blanked, although I knew I hadn't done anything wrong.

Considering our poor draw, we did brilliantly on the first day, and we were still in with a chance. A lot of this was down to Denis, who managed to catch a tiny roach on a part of a squatt just a few minutes from the end and get 10 points for it. The Italians had done really well from peg 1 using a method they use a lot, but one that has only recently been seen in England – the Bolognese style. They had only 20 points while we had 61 and were fifth. But it was the sort of water where you could easily drop a lot of points with a poor draw – as the next day proved.

We thought we had a better draw on the next day, peg 7, though it was hard to say what a better draw was. Still, the Hungarians had been on that peg the previous day, had never practised on the water and still came third, so we were hopeful. I was in a peg that had blanked the previous day, but I felt that I might sneak a fish or two. You have to approach matches like this in a confident state of mind, otherwise you are beaten before you start.

I did exactly the same as on the previous day, but after 30 minutes my float went down and I hooked a bream.

I've never taken so long to land a bream in my life. The next one 10 minutes later came in a lot quicker, because I knew I'd got those vital points. But I had to wait until 30 minutes from the end before I got my third fish. I had one more bite where I felt the fish, which was another bream, but it wouldn't have made any difference. We finished fourth, amazingly beaten by the Channel Islands, fishing their first match. With no disrespect to them, it says a great deal about what a lottery the match was. The Italians won, but even the great Milo Colombo couldn't catch a fish on the second day. And for us, both Tommy and Kevin blanked that day, surely the only time in the history of the World Championship that Kevin hasn't had a fish.

For him and me not to catch a fish in Ireland is incredible. But it was a disastrous venue. Even Yugoslavia was nowhere near as bad as that. Italy won with 94 points, which must be the highest total ever to win a World Championship. They did this despite two dry nets on the second day. France were just behind with 96. We had 125 points and came fourth, beaten by the Channel Islands. Several anglers never had a bite on either day, including a couple of the Australians. Fancy coming all that way for two blanks.

Afterwards, there was a lot of publicity about the Bolognese style of floatfishing, and speculation that England should have fished with it on the first day, when conditions were perfect for it and several teams, notably the Italians, picked up fish using it. We all had Bolognese rods with us, but we stuck with the slider because we had not found that Bolognese gave us any advantage on that water. It's true that it enabled the bait to be in your swim a little longer, but during practice we had found that even when it was moving through, the bream would still take – as long as they were in the peg. On the second day of the match, Milo searched the whole river and ended up fishing three-quarters of the way across, but even he couldn't get a fish. Bolognese is a terrific method, but it can't catch you fish when they're not there. You also have to consider that it was a very new method to us, whereas the Italians are very skilled with it. If we had all fished against them on Bolognese, we wouldn't have beaten them because they've been doing it all their lives. The one good thing – perhaps the only good thing, except for 21-year-old Dave Wesson of Australia winning the individual title – to come out of that match was the popularizing of Bolognese. Since we came back, tackle shops in England have been inundated with requests for the rods. I think it will become a key method over the next decade.

4

WINNING ON THE POLE

*T*he World Championships have been the highlight of my angling career, but as my fishing has improved there have been some other good wins along the way. I would still love to win a National, but fishing in the top division against 1,000 anglers, most of whom are pretty good, means that your chances of doing so are quite slim. I don't think I've even drawn in an area where I've had a chance to shine yet, but each year I turn up thinking that maybe this will be my year.

A water I don't want to remember: Plovdiv in Bulgaria, 1989. I just didn't learn the obvious lesson.

Since the 1982 win by Essex County, I've never been in a winning National team, although we've come close on a couple of occasions. The most recent was on the Witham in 1990, one of the fairest Nationals I've ever fished. We came fourth, but we didn't work as hard on it as we should have done. I had just come back from winning the World Championships, so it's not surprising that my mind wasn't entirely on the National. However, I don't think any team would have beaten Trev's Browning that year. It was a bloodworm and joker match and they knew just what to do. We would have been second but for one terrible result by Jan Porter, who only got four points.

I weighed in 5 lb 10 oz (2.55 kg) and came third in my section, though I didn't catch many fish at the start, as you often do on the Witham. I started in close, and fed a 12 yd (m) line. I didn't realize how many fish were in my peg, so I didn't put enough feed in. My own fault for not practising! I was catching a few small fish on 4 m to hand, feeding little balls of groundbait, but it was hard and I was on course for only about 2 lb (900 g).

I'd fished for about 90 minutes and only had about 10 oz (285 g) in the net. When I went out, it wasn't much better, but instinct made me up the feed slowly, and the more I put in just loose joker, the better the fishing became. I was feeding joker with just a tiny bit of groundbait to hold it together, and in the last hour I had about 4 lb (1.80 kg) of quality roach. I sat on my box afterwards thinking: 'Why didn't I know that? Why didn't I do that earlier?' But it was all down to practice.

I wasn't sure if the eels would feed. You can't put in joker and groundbait, then loosefeed over the top and expect to catch eels. It doesn't work because eels steer clear of groundbait. You have to put maggots even further out, at least 2-3 metres clear of your bloodworm line. Although eels will take bloodworm, they don't like groundbait. So the decision was whether to go for eels, which meant loosefeeding, or to fish for the roach and skimmers. I got the method right, but too late. And eels didn't show on the day, which wrecked the team plan of quite a few sides that had based their strategy around them.

If I had been on the water more, I would have known that I could attack it. By the end, I had fed 3 pt (1.5 litre) of joker and my swim was full of fish. As it was, I took it cautiously because I didn't want to overfeed, and I failed to take full advantage of the peg. Another pound, and I would have had my first National section win.

However, winning a National individual title is a bit of a lottery. I suspect it's more prestigious to win a contest like the UK Championships, which during its existence has been variously called the Whitbread and the MacPhersons Championships. These matches started in 1985 and the idea was that 60 of the country's top matchmen would fish four waters in different parts of the country. The event is decided on section points over the four matches. With the winner collecting up to £5,000, almost every leading matchman takes part. You know that you have done really well if you even win your section. It is a much fairer reflection of the UK champion than any National can be.

It's an event that has generally been very kind to me. In the first year I came seventh, and I could have done even better except for one disastrous result. I've been third, fourth and I won the series in 1986. I even won a match that was part of the 1988 series, even though I didn't have any tackle at the time! It happened because we had been practising for the World Championships and my tackle hadn't arrived back in time. This match was on the Trent at Holme Marsh, and I only fished because Frank Barlow's son Dean lent me some tackle. It's the only time, except in those very early days, that I've turned up to a match with just one rod.

I was obviously meant to win that day. I fished stick float, which was all I could do, and caught 9 lb (4.1 kg) of roach and an 11 lb (5 kg) pike that took bronze maggot. I was convinced it was a carp because it charged upstream for about six pegs. It's almost the largest fish I've ever had on a match, though I once landed a 14 lb (6.35 kg) carp at Layer pits. I'm not totally convinced that pike should count in matches, but I had no complaints that day!

Still, winning one of the matches is very different from finishing first after four events. You need to draw well, it's true, but you've also got to fish very well against all the England team anglers and pretty well everyone who is on the fringes of the team, too. That's why I was so delighted to win the 1986 series, dropping just two points over the four matches.

THE 1986 UK CHAMPIONSHIPS

The first contest was on the Witham, and it was going to be an eel match. I don't particularly like eels, but obviously we had to fish for them. I was practising the night before and getting loads of bites. The more bites I missed, the more I fed and the more bites I got. The float was flying everywhere and I couldn't get one. Then Wayne Swinscoe, whom I knew fairly well, came along. He told me I was feeding far too heavily. I had everything else right,

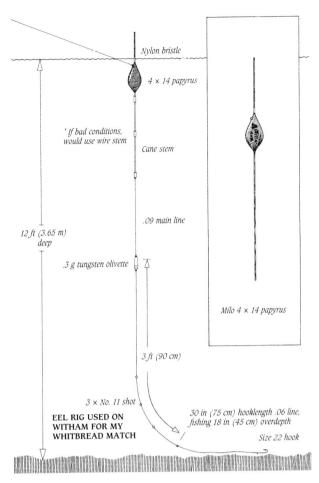

Nylon bristle

4 × 14 papyrus

If bad conditions, would use wire stem

Cane stem

.09 main line

12 ft (3.65 m) deep

.3 g tungsten olivette

Milo 4 × 14 papyrus

3 ft (90 cm)

3 × No. 11 shot

EEL RIG USED ON WITHAM FOR MY WHITBREAD MATCH

30 in (75 cm) hooklength .06 line, fishing 18 in (45 cm) overdepth

Size 22 hook

hooks and all that, but Wayne told me to feed as if I was after a few roach, and just to put in seven or eight maggots at a time. I had been feeding a pouch-full every cast!

I had no chance to try it out because I had already ruined the peg. I had to trust Wayne, and hope he was telling the truth. The next day it was very warm and slow moving, ideal conditions for eels. Alan Scothorne of Barnsley won with 13 lb 10 oz 12 dr (6.206 kg) of skimmers, but I was second and won my section with 7 lb 13 oz 8 dr (3.552 kg) of eels, the biggest weight of eels I've ever had in a match. Wayne had put me exactly right and helped me towards the £5,000 given as prize money. I had 34 eels, mostly 3-4 oz (85-115 g).

I was fishing on the pole at 10 metres with a long tail and a size 22 hook. I had designed something to help me unhook the eels – a big bowl of dry groundbait – so I was putting them into this as I swung them in. It meant they were very easy to unhook, and it worked brilliantly. I

pulled my net out at the end and I was puzzled at all the groundbait inside it. 'That's funny,' I said to someone, 'I haven't been using groundbait.' Then I remembered!

The second match of the series was at Dryad Lake in Portsmouth, and I looked upon it almost as my home venue, though it is actually more than 100 miles from my home. The reason I liked it so much was that it involved carp fishing, and I just love fishing for them. After years on Layer pits in Colchester, I really knew how to catch carp. Earlier that season, I had won a big series at Dryad.

The lake is inside the naval base. It's long and narrow, more like a river, and only 3-4 ft (1-1.2 m) deep. It was full of carp up to 3 lb (1.35 kg). The year before, I had devised this terrific way of catching them. It was an adaptation of the method I had used at Layer pits, where you could put heavy balls of groundbait in and keep feeding until the carp turned up. You didn't need to fish out too far at Dryad – a ½ oz (15 g) bomb would easily get you to the middle – but anglers were pegged on either side of the lake. You really wanted to draw in the middle.

The prevailing wind usually blew down the lake from the west, and the secret was to concentrate your feed. I had discovered that the answer was to use very sloppy groundbait packed with pinkies and floating casters. I put a soft ball in with every cast and threw my lead on top of it, fishing with a 5 ft (1.5 m) tail and two floating maggots. In the early Dryad days, I was the only one doing this, and by the end of the match I had virtually the whole population of the lake in my peg. The people on either side of me were benefiting a little because they were picking off odd ones, but they could never compete. I won loads of matches using this method, catching those carp that were feeding on the top on those floating casters. So I knew exactly what to do, and I told Wayne as a thank-you for putting me right on the previous match.

The match day was scarcely a good one for carp fishing. It was dull, cold and miserable, and so I adapted the method. I realized that in such conditions the carp wouldn't come to the top, but would go to the bottom for the pinkies. Everything else would happen just the same, but you wouldn't see them because they were all on the bottom. By then, everybody had learned about my method of fishing on the top, but I fished on the bottom that day! I was confident that wherever I drew, I was going to do well. However, I drew down one end of the lake, and I was very fortunate to win.

I wasn't fishing very far out, but I fed a lot, including nearly 1 gallon (4.5 litre) of old casters. The pinkies and a few sinking casters were going down to the bottom, but the floaters were drifting off on the wind. The fish, however, came up to find the source, just as they do on a river. And they ended up right where the feed was going in. At the end, I was firing a ball and could see all these backs coming out of the water where they were going for it.

I shouldn't have won from my position. The difference was that I didn't lose the fish I hooked. I caught 15 fish, all on treble pinkie, and only lost a couple, weighing in 31 lb 9 oz (14.316 kg), just ahead of Stan Piecha with 30 lb 12 oz (13.940 kg). Almost every angler was telling stories about how many bites he'd missed, and how many fish he'd lost. My experience of playing big fish on small hooks and very light lines at Layer pits was the perfect training for a water like Dryad. The important thing with carp is never to strike, but just to lift up the rod and backwind. You don't worry about little line bites. Your rod goes right round, you pick it up and they're on. Striking with 1 lb (450 g) line and a size 22 hook is a recipe for disaster.

I had told Kevin Ashurst what to do as well as Wayne, who finished second in his section. But Kevin changed his mind and tried to fish with casters. He still weighed in about 15 lb (6.8 kg), but lost 10 fish and tried to step up his tackle when he started losing them. Carp fishing can be very deceptive, even for the very best anglers!

FISHING THE LEAD

It's strange that a lot of anglers don't believe I even own a leger rod, but I've won a lot of money on the lead. However well you master the pole, there are going to be times when you have to go on the lead. You can't leger in the World Championships and it seems very unlikely that it will ever be allowed. However, anyone aspiring to become a top match angler must master the two main methods: the feeder and the bomb.

People think I never fish the feeder, but I use both the open feeder and maggot feeder quite a lot. I like the round, green maggot feeders best, but I always adapt the holes on shop-bought models. I enlarge them with a pair of scissors because I want the feed to come out quickly. Larger holes also prevent false bites caused by the fish trying to take maggots that get stuck in the holes. Ideally when you cast in, some of the bait should come out as the feeder sinks, which helps to draw fish to your hookbait. You certainly don't want maggots still in the feeder when you wind in.

On running water, I use the loop method of attaching the feeder, with the feeder on a loop of about 15 in (37.5 cm). To prevent tangles, tie a loop in this of about 2½ in (6.2 cm), and a tiny loop in this smaller loop. The hook length is attached to the tiniest loop.

It is important to get the weight right. The rig should not be anchored to the bottom because it should move if a fish takes. The weight should be just enough to hold bottom. The bites will generally be drop-backs. I vary the length of the tail a lot. When fishing for chub, you can sometimes come really short, to about 6 in (15 cm). And if you are getting bites quickly and not seeing them, you must shorten down.

If you are casting a long way with a feeder, you need a 5 lb (2.5 kg) shock leader and 2½ or 3 lb (1 or 1.5 kg) main line. I generally use Maxima because it's a good sinking line and very robust. The problem with using 5 lb (2.5 kg) straight through is that you need to use more lead to hold bottom. It's better to use as thin a reel line as you can, to minimize water pressure on the line.

Even in winter, I don't bother to tape up the holes on my feeder, as some anglers do. I just cut down the number of maggots I put in, or use a smaller feeder. I like the maggot feeder for carp, especially in clear water. I prefer it to the groundbait feeder in most cases because carp seem attracted to large quantities of maggots.

Wherever I am likely to catch a lot of fish, I usually use a large feeder, cast it out and retrieve it almost immediately for several casts to lay down a carpet of bait. The feeder is brilliant for feeding at distance in one spot — but you must learn to be accurate.

Unless I am catching fish such as carp that I am going to have to backwind on, I always use the line clip on the reel spool. This means that once I have decided where I am going to fish, I set the line round the clip and forget about it. I can be certain that my feeder will finish in exactly the same spot every time. You also need to pick out a target opposite you to ensure you are not only casting out the same distance, but on the same line as well. Even if you are fishing at 50 yd (m) or more, you know that your feeder is within 1 ft (30 cm) of where it was last time.

This is great for one's confidence. I was fishing like this recently at Ten Mile Bank, chucking right across. After about four or five casts, I started to get bites. I knew that I could continue to cast into the area where the fish were feeding, rather than trying to guess whether I was in the right spot. We often think that our feeder is landing spot-on, but it's easy to be several yards out when you're fishing very long. If the feeder deviated from the straight by 1 m, I'd pull it back before it did any damage.

Many reels now have line clips included. You can use an elastic band instead, but it's not so good because it sometimes catches as you cast out. You can still cast exactly to the spot if you are fishing two lines as well. I use a sliding knot for the short line, and use the line clip for my distance swim. I was fishing the feeder in Ireland in about 35 ft (10.65 m) of water and it was vital to get into exactly the same spot each cast. To begin with I was catching the occasional bream, but as the match progressed I was catching more and more, while those around me were not catching so well. It was all because my hookbait and feed were landing in exactly the same area.

On the 1992 Ulster Classic, I drew at Rosscarne next to Bill Bywater, an excellent bream angler, on the second day. I knew it had been fishing hard, so I didn't feed any groundbait, just what went in through the feeder. I decided where I was going to fish, cast out and put the line clip on. My swim had an uneven bottom so I was fishing double caster, with one of the casters buried so the hook wouldn't catch on the bottom. I won the section easily with 44 lb (20 kg) and the next weight was about 15 lb 8 oz (7 kg).

I never use the line clip when I'm fishing for carp because they often take so hard and fast that they will break you if you leave the line clip on. You never need to strike carp; just pick the rod up and backwind, and let them run unless there are bad obstructions nearby.

A lot of anglers just cast out, and then decide that's where they'll fish. But it's just as important to work out your depths on the lead as it is on a float line, and once again, the line clip can come in useful. You are generally not allowed to cast out a feeder before a match, but you can use a bomb to find out the depths, and this is what I do. Cast to the area you think you want to fish, and count how many seconds the bomb takes to hit bottom. Work around the peg, and you will soon have an idea of the shelves and gullies. When you have a good idea where you want to fish, cast out to that spot and set your line clip. Now you can put your feeder on and be certain from the very first cast that you will be on the right spot.

You don't have to cast to the clip, although it doesn't matter if you do in shallow waters. In deep water, however, cast slightly shorter, feathering your line, and the depth will take the line out to the clip.

When using an open or groundbait feeder, I use a light mix: brown crumb mixed with Van den Eynde Active Feeder. The feeder travels fairly quickly to the bottom and as soon as it hits the deck, particles explode out of it. Drop a little groundbait on the bottom close in and you can see

it work. It gets the fish interested; it's not just lying there inactive. If you watch your rod top carefully (I always use a quivertip of 11 or 12 ft (3.35 or 3.65 m) so it will cast a big feeder and pick up plenty of line), you can spot just a slight movement as the feeder empties. Keep your mix fairly dry. The wetter it is, the harder and the longer it will stay in. You should never be winding back and finding half your groundbait still in the feeder.

It's amazing how little groundbait you actually need inside a feeder to put out a lot of bait such as casters or hemp. I learnt this from Malcolm Taylor of A4, whose side have really got the feeder down to a fine art. The groundbait can be a handful of crushed hemp, a little brown crumb and 1 pt (500 ml) of casters. It's virtually all caster. This is an easy way to put 1-2 pints (500 ml-1 litre) of casters in the peg, and that's brilliant for chub, which prefer the caster to lots of groundbait.

I use clear plastic feeders most of the time, except when I'm really going for distance. Then I'll put on a frame feeder, which is just the thing when you are casting 80 or 90 metres.

When the fish are reacting well, and as long as you can feed by hand or don't want to feed at all, the bomb is much faster. Sometimes when you are feeder fishing, the fish will go off a bit. It can be that they are getting wary of the feeder, but a bomb will still catch them.

On the bomb I usually use a paternoster set-up rather than the loop. If you go on the straight lead, you are probably looking to catch fish on the drop and the paternoster enables you to catch anywhere in that last 6 ft (1.8 m) of drop. This is especially so in some of the southern Irish lakes for roach. It works very well with a swingtip, which is still a superb method because there is no resistance. When I'm fishing for skimmers, I often use a target board. Skimmers hardly move the tip at times and you have to strike every tiny indication. I find that I usually start with a tail of 3-4 ft (1-1.2 m).

Although I do most of my fishing on a pole, I'm not afraid to put a bomb on the same line. This happens particularly if the wind is so strong that I can't hold the pole still, and can't put a float through properly. Sometimes the fish will drop just out of pole range, and you can follow them on a bomb. In this instance I would fish a very light main line, perhaps 1½ lb (680 g), with a little lead that just held bottom.

Legering had paid dividends in that second match of the Whitbread UK Championships series, and I had made a terrific start – two section wins, and a first and second overall. But I was worried about the third match, which was on Carr Mill Dam at St Helens. It was a patchy water and I had no time to practise. The target fish were skimmers, but the fishing was nearly all on the pole, which suited me fine. It was a local water for Kevin, who told me roughly how to fish it. However, I drew badly and ended up towards the top end, where the wind was off my back and the water was 6 ft (1.8 m) deep. It's not a good area, but all the pegs to the right of me were bad as well, so at least I was competing on fairly even terms.

I fished with a long pole and short line and fed sloppy groundbait and squatts. The fish never went mad, but I finished with 5 lb (2.25 kg) of little skimmers on squatts. I was beaten at the next peg by John Allerton of Barnsley, who knows the water very well, but he only just pipped me with 5 lb 2 oz (2.810 kg). He won the section and I was second. I never had a chance in the match overall, but getting second in my section kept me on top of the leader board. Still, there were only two points separating me and the England team manager, Dick Clegg, and the final match was on the Embankment stretch of the Trent at Nottingham, which could be considered his home water.

The Embankment is a water that responds to the pole, because there were plenty of small fish there close in. And the peg I drew was ideal. I had a steady run-through at 10 metres, where it was 6 ft (1.8 m) deep. I just fed bronze maggot and a bit of hemp, used a small float and caught loads of gudgeon and small roach to weigh in 12 lb 3 oz 12 dr (5.546 kg). The match, almost inevitably, was won on the waggler, but I finished second in my section again, fifth in the match and that £5,000 top prize was mine. Because I'd had a win and a second, those four matches brought me a total of more than £6,500.

Perhaps most satisfying was that, except for the Dryad match, I'd done it all on the pole. I was convinced then that pole fishing was the future of angling, and I still am. So maybe this is a good place to talk about pole fishing and how I go about it.

POLE FISHING

The development of the pole has been the greatest advance in angling over the past 20 years, because you can fish lighter tackle, lighter floats and get perfect presentation. Swims that were difficult or impossible to fish, especially on canals, are now easy for a pole angler. You can fish with far finer hooklengths and much smaller hooks than on rod and line, which means that you're going to get more bites and catch more fish. You can use an 8 oz (0.25 kg) breaking strain line, yet land 2 lb (900 g) fish on it if your elastic is set up right.

Pole tackle

Buying a pole can be a daunting experience. It's not easy even for an experienced matchman. Ideally the pole should be fairly stiff, though a pole that's like a poker isn't such a good buy. Even though you will be using elastic to absorb the pulls of a fish, your pole should have a little 'give'. We prefer stiff poles in the UK because the wind is often a factor. The Italians use telescopic poles with a lot of give in them because wind is rarely a problem.

If you are going to be catching a lot of fish, and will be unshipping the pole all the time, put-over sections are best because they fit together more easily. You don't want the joints sticking in wet weather. Anyone who has carried three sections of a tightly jammed pole back to his car will know what I mean! With put-in joints, you tend to get a narrower, lighter pole, more suited for fishing to hand or in Ireland. Put-in poles are also generally stronger.

There is no longer an easy way of telling a pole's quality. You can squeeze a light pole gently to see if it has acquired that lightness from being ultra-thin, and therefore potentially weak. But the best way is to see what poles the top anglers are using. You can be sure that they will go for the best.

Only a couple of years ago, 11 m was the accepted length. Then it went up to 12.5 m, and now everybody seems to feel that they must have a 14 m model. It will probably be 16 m before very long. I've just taken delivery of a new Browning 16.5 m pole, which I suppose is the shape of things to come. But this obsession with length can be counter-productive. I love fishing at 11 and 12 m, and while I can handle more than 17 m, I would hate to fish at this length all day. There are times when you need to put the odd couple of joints on, but most pegs can easily be covered at 10-12 m.

Of course there are a few pegs, particularly on canals, where the ability to poke a pole right against a bed of rushes or under a bush will bring bonus fish. When the Grand Union Canal at Three Locks was fishing well on caster, we battled to get a waggler to hold across as the wind would pull it out of the peg in a few seconds. Now you can drop a caster under a little pole float right on the spot and hold it out there as long as you like.

I think even a club matchman should buy at least one 'extra top-three' kit, giving you a duplicate of the three thinnest sections. Most open matchmen now have at least two extra top-three kits, and perhaps a top-five kit as well. If you are fishing water that's 12 ft (3.65 m) deep, a top-three kit won't give you enough length for a spare rig. You can't leave a top-three on the bank for such swims without the probability of it getting caught in bankside vegetation or tangled in wind.

The English took a long time to learn about poles, but we've been making up for that by developing perhaps the most important aspect of pole fishing – elastication. We threaded it on the outside to start with. I remember putting rings on my pole and running the elastic through, but you get a lot of friction that way. By far the best way is to thread elastic through the pole's centre.

Now the Continentals, who taught us the potential of pole fishing, are copying us. We even export PTFE bushes, which fit in the end of the pole, to Italy. I prefer internal micro bushes because there's nothing for the line to catch on. The bush actually fits inside the pole, but because it is so small I only have to lose about 2 in (5 cm) off the pole to fit it. The Stonfo connectors for the end of the elastic have got smaller too, and their weight is no longer a problem, although I don't use Stonfo connectors except for No. 6 and No. 8 elastic, because of the risk of the Stonfo flicking over the pole. The diagram illustrates how I connect the elastic. It's a system I designed about two years ago and it works perfectly.

I use Preston Innovations' colour-coded elastics, which are impregnated to make them less abrasive. Like car tyres, elastic shouldn't slip. You have to lubricate it so it will run backwards and forwards. If it starts to stick, you will get jerky movements and 'bump' fish. I treat the elastic with a silicon-based lubricant that needs to be re-applied every time I fish. It goes inside the pole, but not from the bush end. If elastic hangs out of the pole, this is usually

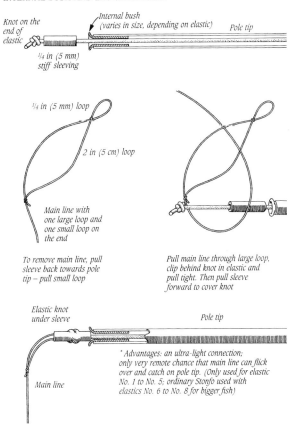

INTERNAL BUSH AND END CONNECTION

Knot on the end of elastic

Internal bush (varies in size, depending on elastic)

Pole tip

1/4 in (5 mm) stiff sleeving

1/4 in (5 mm) loop

2 in (5 cm) loop

Main line with one large loop and one small loop on the end

To remove main line, pull sleeve back towards pole tip – pull small loop

Pull main line through large loop, clip behind knot in elastic and pull tight. Then pull sleeve forward to cover knot

Elastic knot under sleeve

Pole tip

Main line

*Advantages: an ultra-light connection; only very remote chance that main line can flick over and catch on pole tip. (Only used for elastic No. 1 to No. 5; ordinary Stonfo used with elastics No. 6 to No. 8 for bigger fish)

caused by water being drawn back in with the elastic, which then sticks. Silicone lubricant stops this.

The chart shows the relationship between the elastic used, the number of sections that it runs through and the end tackle. It's vital for a matchman to understand this, and to be certain that he is using the right elastic and rig.

Preston Innovations' elastics and using balanced tackle with them

CODE NUMBER	COLOUR	ELASTIC DIAMETER	POLE SECTIONS	MAIN LINE (TYPICAL)	HOOKLENGTH (TYPICAL)	HOOK SIZE	MAIN USES
1	Purple	0.58	One	0.06	0.05	24-26	Shallow canals
2	Red	0.67	Two	0.07	0.05-06	22-26	Deeper canals, stillwater
3	Green	0.75	Two	0.07	0.05-06	22-26	Stillwater, canals with more fish
4	Orange	0.85	Two	0.08	0.06-07	20-24	Stillwater, slow rivers
5	Blue	0.91	Two	0.09	0.07-08	18-22	Stillwater with more fish, slow rivers
6	Yellow	1.06	Three	0.09-10	0.07-08	18-22	Stillwater, small carp, running water
8	Grey	1.27	Three	0.10-16	0.08-14	14-20	Hard-running rivers, carp, tench etc

I haven't included typical floats in this, but obviously use of the correct float is critical to ensure balanced tackle. For example, you wouldn't use a 1 g float with No. 2 elastic and a 24.

Catching carp on the pole at Decoy Lakes.

A No. 1 elastic is the finest you can get. You can only really put that through one section because it is so fine that if you stretch it through two, you won't have enough pull to return it. Use No. 1 on shallow canals, when you're fishing with very small hooks and catching very small fish with perhaps the odd bonus fish. If you use too thick an elastic in this situation, you run the risk of bumping them on that tiny hook.

You can get virtually the same effect by stretching a No. 2 elastic through two sections. I can't think of a use for No. 1 that cannot be duplicated better by No. 2. It gives the same silky smoothness, but because the elastic is running through two sections, you've got a bit of extra 'give' if you hook a bonus fish. No. 2 elastic through two sections is about right for most canal fishing if you're using blood-worm and small baits, and not expecting bonus fish too often. If you are using baits such as caster, a No. 3 elastic through two sections is better to set the slightly larger hook, or if you are catching a lot of fish and want to get them in that bit quicker.

On rivers, where you will be using larger floats and where you may want to lift more fish, it's time to start thinking about a No. 4, again through two sections. You might even have to use a No. 5. Above this, I start to run my elastic through three sections. If you're on a river and it's hard going, but you're netting most fish, then No. 5 is all right. But if you're looking at an 18 or 20 hook and lifting 2 oz (56 g) fish, then it's time to go up to a No. 6.

There isn't a No. 7, so it's on to No. 8, which I run through three sections as well. No. 8 is extra strong and thick, but you can still catch 2 oz fish with it without bumping them, and lift them straight in, as I did in the World Championship in Hungary. On that occasion I was using a No. 8 elastic and catching 2-3 oz (56-85 g) roach on a size 20 hook, with the occasional 1 lb (450 g) fish as well. No. 8 is the highest I go. There's no advantage, as far as I'm concerned, in using No. 9.

The biggest carp I can get out is about 8 lb (3.6 kg) on No. 8 elastic through three sections, with 0.16 main line of about 4 lb (1.8 kg) breaking strain. You might think that the answer would be to put the elastic through five sections, but it wouldn't make any difference. The elastic still bottoms out and you are back to the old problem of being unable to control the fish.

It is not easy to set up the correct tension for elastic. I always tend to err on the side of under-tensioning; in other words, so that it looks as if the elastic is not slipping back inside the pole very well. New elastic always takes a bit of time to set in so never over-tighten it, always go the other way. It might take a little time to trickle back in, particularly on the softer brands, but it shouldn't bang straight back inside the pole. That sort of effect usually results in bumped fish, because you strike and the elastic wants to spring back immediately.

Although I have six tips for my poles, I still sometimes have to change elastics. I usually leave my thick ones, No. 6 and No. 8, permanently set up, but I change the other four all the time. This is not something you want to do on the bank, even though it's quite easy with the new threaders. It's all down to preparation, a word I keep repeating.

I check the light elastics every trip for signs of wear. The place to look is by the knot or Stonfo. I change elastic whenever I spot the slightest sign of wear. A No. 8 will probably last all season, provided that you're not catching carp every day, but the finer elastics can wear quickly. The other routine maintenance I carry out is to treat my pole ferrules with a liquid called Jointsave. Carbon to carbon is very abrasive. It's like rubbing two sheets of sandpaper together, so it's no wonder that joints wear. This liquid puts a seal on the carbon and takes off some of the abrasiveness.

Occasionally I will fish without elastic on the long pole. I use a heavy flick tip for aggressive fishing in Ireland, even when I'm using a long pole with short line. I might then be using 5 lb (2.25 kg) main line, 4 lb (1.80 kg) hooklength and a size 12 hook so I can swing 8-10 oz (225-283 g) roach to hand. There's no elastic made that I know of that can swing 8 oz (225 g) fish.

I don't use a soft flick tip any more. I prefer to fish elastic, because when I strike I can fling the pole behind me and the elastic will fly out of the end of the pole without the hook tearing from a fish's mouth. With a flick tip you have to be more careful. It can be an advantage in really windy conditions, when you bury the tip underwater and hold back. But given the developments in elastic, I think the flick tip for light work is now outmoded. The method I have become best known for is long pole, short line. And I suppose the question I get asked most is what distance should there be between the top of the pole and the float.

There isn't a simple answer to this. It depends where you are fishing and how precisely you want to fish. Sometimes you need the float a little way away from the pole, particularly on shallow or clear water where the pole may frighten the fish. On rivers, it's always best to have quite a bit of line between pole and tip because you want to run down the peg. It could be as much as 3 metres. On somewhere like the Gloucester Canal, which is very uneven and slopes very steeply, you need to be very precise. Then you want a really short line with the float right under your tip so you are fishing in the same spot every time.

Many people shorten up if it's windy, but that's the wrong thing to do. If it's really windy, it's better to use a bit more line and backshot your float. The closer the distance between your pole and float, the more you will move that float in the wind. On a canal float, you only need a tiny backshot, but remember to take one shot from below the float to compensate.

The other question I am always asked about is how many metres should one fish to hand? Again, there isn't a right answer until you know what depth you are dealing with. Obviously the more sections you have to unship, the longer it's going to take, so ideally you want to unship as few sections as possible and still keep control.

It's easy to get stereotyped. I won several matches in Ireland in 1992 by fishing not to hand but long pole, short line. Fishing to hand would have meant a bigger float and I would have been missing bites. I won two matches with nearly 60 lb (27.2 kg), netting almost everything.

Pole fishing on canals

However, Ireland's a very special case. Far more common is use of the long pole, short line on still waters or a canal. Let's take the Grand Union Canal in West Drayton, about 20 miles outside London, which is fairly typical. You have three lines to fish, sometimes four. There is a near-shelf swim; just over the shelf on the near side; the bottom of the far shelf; and perhaps on top of the far shelf, too.

This far shelf can produce some surprisingly big fish: carp, chub, big roach and perch. It is often the warmest place, and in summer, fish find it the best place to get out of the way of boats. Boat traffic always pushes fish to the extremes. Although boats can be a problem and some anglers get very upset about them, they give canals a bit of colour and play a big part in stopping them silting up. There are always inconsiderate boat-owners who charge along the canal and disperse your feed everywhere. You don't want that to keep happening with light feed and joker. Sometimes it's a good idea to feed just after a boat has gone through, because the boat's noise is still in the background and that groundbait going in won't cause quite as much disturbance.

In summer, bottom weed is often a problem, so you have to fish just above the weed, particularly if you're using bloodworm. The lesson is to plumb carefully. I try to find a clear hole in the weed. I don't use special plummets for canals, just small ones.

If I'm fishing off the bottom, I usually use a slim-bodied float with a wire bristle and wire stem. The wire stem gives stability and the bristle sensitivity. Perch bites often hardly move the float, although you can sometimes see the float tremble.

On West Drayton in the summer, 7 lb (3.15 kg) is a good weight. The fish usually come on the 5-6 metre line, where it is just going down the shelf. Getting them this close means you can flick tiny bits of joker on top of the float. But even in the summer, when fish are more active, you've still got to feed three swims and not hit any of them too hard. You might catch five fish off your close lines, then go across for a couple more. It doesn't matter when you switch, as long as you don't wait until a swim is completely dead. As soon as you are starting to wait for bites, leave

that swim and go across. Give the catching swim a rest – but remember to keep feeding it.

For this style of fishing, I use very light floats. I take the original wire out and replace it with a heavier wire, so the float changes from 4 × 11 to 4 × 12, and will only take 0.1 g down the line. I usually use shot because they give more flexibility than styls for changing the presentation.

My main line is usually 0.07. In summer I use 0.06 hook-lengths, and 0.05 in the winter. It will always be a high-tech line because your hook line must be soft. Canal fish are naturally more wary and harder to catch. A very light hooklength ensures that the bait behaves as naturally as possible. I use quite a large hook for bloodworm. My favourite is a fine-wire green barbless Kamakatsu. I know it seems odd to use a barbless hook for bloodworm, but these hooks are incredibly sharp and as long as you use soft elastic and keep the tension on, particularly when fishing for perch, you will retain the fish.

As long as the canal has a tinge of colour and the pole is not affecting the fish, I generally fish with 18-24 in (45-60 cm) between float and tip. If it's windy, I'll fish a bit longer and backshot.

When it comes to feeding, I generally put two tangerine-sized balls on my close-in line and perhaps six on a middle line. On the far bank I feed a tiny touch of grey leam with some raw joker. It will stick together enough to throw raw joker up to 16 yd (m). You still have the option of loosefeeding casters on top, and when you go out there, you can fish bloodworm or caster.

On a line that's going down the shelf, I would put in a cup of chopped worm, especially when there are perch about. It doesn't damage the swim at all, but tends to lie there longer than joker will, giving you the chance to pick

A very long pole will produce big bream like this more consistently. They seem to prefer living a few yards off the shelf.

up a big perch later in the match. This works particularly well in winter, but it is still a good summer method. In fact, sometimes you can't get a bite on bloodworm and yet chopped worm will bring fish.

Chopped worm

Chopped worm has become a premier method when bloodworm is banned. It works on the same principle as a small container of worm extract called Ace, which relies on fish being attracted to the smell of worms. And they certainly are! I'll happily put chopped worm over joker, winter or summer.

I know some people use lobworms, but I prefer large redworms. I usually take a couple of tubs with me, but I wouldn't expect to use them all. I use a pair of sharp scissors and keep chopping them until they are in pieces between ¼ and ½ in (6-12 mm) long. I don't add anything to them; they just go in raw.

With this approach you are usually looking to catch perch, ruffe or gudgeon, though I've had roach up to 14 oz (395 g) on it. On canals, perch are often in different areas to other fish. You might even catch them in the channel in the middle of winter. But in general, cup some in on a near swim and a far swim.

Often on canals where bloodworm is barred, you may be looking to catch early fish on the punch. You don't want to mix chopped worm with that. You might attract big perch, which will frighten fish off your punch line.

You want a slightly heavier rig for chopped worm, perhaps 0.3 g. The worm itself is quite a heavy bait, so you don't want to use a wire bristle. Because you often want to lay the worm on the bottom and drag it one way or the other, the float should have the more buoyant cane or nylon bristle.

I still use shots rather than an olivette, perhaps six No. 12s down the line, but I might put some together. With chopped worm, the fish are generally taking on the bottom, so I usually pull three or four together and have two droppers below this. The nearest one would be about 8 in (20 cm) from the hook. You can get away with a slightly larger hook, perhaps a 22 or even a 20, but it will be fine wire, coupled with a No. 2 elastic. A lot of the fish will only be the same size as your bloodworm fish. Perch of 2 oz (56 g) are bonus fish.

My favourite bait is the reddish part of the tail from a small redworm. The smaller worms are more active when you break them. Hook it through the broken end and it will wriggle so well that you can't imagine any fish refusing

it. Thread it on just as you would a caster, so your hook is partly out of view. The good thing about this is that you don't miss too many bites. If you hook a biggish worm through the middle, it can attract small fish which don't take the bait properly. Often it results in lost or bumped fish. But a small section gets nearly every bite.

I usually start just 2-3 in (5-7.5 cm) overdepth. Those perch are picking up chopped worm on the bottom, not dancing in midwater. The key thing with chopped worm is to keep that bait on the move. Drag it one way, then the other. Make it a gradual movement. The bait itself has plenty of movement, but perch love a moving bait.

Be careful not to overfeed. The only way to feed worm is to cup it in; don't put it in groundbait. The feed is quite heavy, so you know within an area of a square ft where your feed is. Start with two or three cups (I use my 2-in diameter cup), then perhaps top up with half a cup.

Worm is a brilliant bait for bigger fish, and bonus fish, perch of 12 oz (340 g) or more, often turn up. I don't change my rig if I start to get big fish, because I'm confident of landing a 12 oz (340 g) perch on 0.05 line. If you hit one of those golden days when there are fish between 1 and 2 lb (450-900 g) in your peg, you may have to go a little heavier. But perch don't snag you like tench or carp, which is a good thing because perch quite often live near obstructions or close to the bankside. The most prolific area may be right on the far bank, alongside a bush or boat. They are not always in the deepest bit of water. At Willow Park in the summer, the perch tend to be very close in, just down the first shelf.

But back to canals in general. For groundbait, I prefer a mix of Van den Eynde International River and a little bit of Surface. It clouds up to attract fish, but doesn't feed them. I'd mix them fairly moist and run them through a riddle. Because Continental groundbaits have preservatives in them, never leave jokers in your feed as it will kill them. Only add the joker when you are ready to feed.

I run my joker through water before I leave home so they are very active, then mix them with damp leam to separate them. This actually sticks to the joker and helps them to sink. You see a lot of people throwing in joker and half of it floats away. I reckon on 70 per cent leam and joker, and 30 per cent groundbait. Feeding is the hardest thing of all on a canal, and it's very easy to overfeed.

Although you know you are in the same spot when pole fishing, I always pick a marker for my feeding. Without realizing it, you can gradually move round and end up fishing a couple of yards off your feed, so work off a fixed point.

Overfeeding is the most common mistake on this sort of venue. It's always difficult to sort out the approach that will bring the best response from fish, and it will vary from venue to venue, and even from stretch to stretch. On any water, two or three visits are usually needed. The simple rule is to keep each swim topped up. This is particularly so in the summer. You will probably feed your second swim with a pole cup, but you can just flick bits of joker by hand to the near swim. On the far bank, you can loosefeed caster or put a ball of raw joker bound with damp leam across. There's no formula, no secret system. Two balls will not last all day on the far bank, but if there are big fish around, you may want to concentrate on caster rather than joker.

I usually take 750 g-1 kg of joker with me. I don't expect to use it all, but what I don't use will go back into my joker 'aquarium' at home. It's very easy to be tempted to throw in 1 kg of joker just because you've got it beside you, but it won't necessarily catch you more fish and it may fill up those you've got.

I hope things don't reach the stage that they have in France, where they sometimes throw in 5 kg of joker to catch 900 g of fish. But even the French have started to realize that this is ridiculous and are imposing restrictions of around 1 kg. On the European Supercup match at Holme Pierrepont in 1991, some anglers were carrying 8 kg of joker, which is crazy. At shop prices, that's over £100 of bait that is just going to be thrown in the water. I used 3 kg that day because there were so many fish around, and after putting in 900 g, I had to keep topping it up. But that's an exceptional water. Even 1 kg might sound a lot, but remember that when it comes down to it, that's less than 500 ml in each area if you're feeding three swims. That's not much over a five-hour match.

I've been writing a lot about not overfeeding with joker, but I think that an even more common mistake is over-feeding a far-bank swim with casters. You only need to put in six at a time, although that doesn't seem very much and the temptation is to increase the rate to a dozen or more. That's fatal unless it's obvious that the fish are mopping up what you've put in and are clearly hunting for more. A ¼ pt (125 ml) of casters is probably too many for almost any canal match.

Because competitors are limited by what they can set up, I try to choose a rig that will cover me for both caster and bloodworm if I think caster could catch but I'm not certain. I'll put perhaps a 20 hook on and bait with two or three bloodworms, or bury a caster in it. If I start to get a lot of bites on caster, and I'm missing one or two, I'll put a bigger hook on. If I'm getting bites on bloodworm but not catching well, I'll change to a smaller hook.

For the far-bank swim, I generally use a very small float, perhaps only taking three No. 13s, with a wire stem for stability and a cane bristle for visibility. Wire stems are generally best for delicate short-line fishing. With very little weight down the line, you have no olivette to straighten the tackle and cock the float, so you must use wire. If you use a cane or a carbon stem, surface tension can hold a light float up and stop it cocking straight away. But wire, because it's very slim, cuts through the surface tension and cocks faster. The thing you have to beware of with wire stems is the float flicking over when you are shipping out. If your float keeps doing this, throw it away. It's happening because the float is too heavy at the bottom, and the momentum created by shipping out is making it flick over.

In summer you may get bites on the drop from the far bank, but in winter it's often a waiting game. I nearly always fish overdepth (usually about 8 in (20 cm) depending on the actual depth of the water) on the far line.

Bloodworm fishing

Many anglers assume that bloodworm must be fished just off the bottom, and generally that's true. I start between 1 and 3 in (2.5-7.5 cm) off bottom. But in summer, I will often come as much as 2 ft (60 cm) off bottom. If you are flicking in bits of bait every cast, the fish will often rise up

The best fish food of all – raw joker.

and then you can catch at least 6 in (15 cm) off the deck. The other factor that can govern your depth, especially in the summer, is bottom weed.

One of the key things about bloodworm fishing is to keep the bait moving. When I cast in, I'm very happy if my float is picking up the tow on a canal. That movement means I don't have to move the float too much. It's like trotting a river. At other times, you have to lift your float quite high and drop it down, almost as if you are about to cast again. As it goes back in, the float often buries. Keep your bait moving by dragging it one way, then the other. Chopped worm needs the same sort of definite movement. Because my float is set almost at water level, I strike as soon as the float goes. If your tackle is balanced properly, you don't need to wait for the float to bury. In winter, the fishing is similar, but everything is scaled down, with smaller floats and lighter line because you aren't generally going to catch as many fish.

Not all my floats will be ultra-light 0.1 g ones. I may have up to 0.4 g and see which one works best. Sometimes you can get pestered with tiny fish and the heavier rig will get through them. On other occasions, there may be lots of fish in your peg, so fishing with a heavier float enables you to step up your catch rate. A heavier float will always pick up any flow better than a light one, giving you that important movement and enabling you to search the peg better than by continual recasting.

I usually have a light, a medium and a heavy rig set up, both for summer and winter, the winter rig being that bit lighter, with 0.55 line and size 24 hooks. I often use a Browning 282, which is a very fine wire hook with a tiny microbarb. Most anglers feel that on a long pole, short line they have to use at least a microbarb, but using soft elastic and doing everything smoothly, you can get away with a barbless hook and catch much quicker. When you're hooking jokers, barbless hooks can make quite a difference to the time it takes you to bait up.

I never use a pole rest when I'm fishing, except perhaps for baiting up. And I never throw groundbait in without having the pole as a guide, because it's so easy to be 2 ft (50 cm) or more out without realizing it. I put the pole between my legs, holding it with my left hand and throwing the groundbait with my right. Every angler who aspires to success at top level has to practise holding a pole in one hand and feeding with the other, especially at full lengths such as 14 m.

In the summer it's vital to keep bloodworm and joker cool, and direct sunlight will kill them almost immediately.

On very hot days, even maggots can easily get 'cooked'. I carry a cool bag and use bottles of ice to keep my bait in prime condition. Get a few 2-litre lemonade bottles, almost fill them with water and put them in the freezer. They don't cost anything and two can last a day and a half, so your bait will never get too hot.

I fished a match at Wallers Haven in Sussex this year. It was a very hot day, temperatures in the 90s F and we were walking back. Nobody had anything to drink, it was a long walk and we were parched. Them I remembered this bottle of ice. It was still very cold and I was suddenly the most popular man on the bank!

Another system I use to keep bloodworm in peak condition is to roll them in paper. The night before, I pick out my hookers and put them on sheets of moist, but not wet, tissue paper or kitchen roll. Then I put another sheet on top, and put some more on that. I keep the whole lot in a bait box, out of direct sunlight. As I go through a match, every hour I'll take off a sheet and start using the fresh bait below. If it's not too hot, I'll put a little water in a bait box, and add just a touch of raw worm, enough to last me for 20 minutes, and add to it as I use it up. You need to keep bloodworm moist. If you don't, those lovely hookers that you started the match with will shrink to half size, even though they're still alive.

In the winter, you may be feeding for only 1 lb (450 g) of fish. At times like this, the pole cup comes into its own, because it allows you to feed neat joker. Its other advantage is that it allows pinpoint feeding, whether with groundbait or raw joker. If there is some colour in a canal, you can expect to catch roach as well as perch, so groundbait will be all right. If it's gin clear, you probably won't catch as many roach. Perch are likely to be the main species, and that generally means feeding raw joker. Cupping in raw joker is all very well, but it can travel a hell of a long way if there's any movement on the water.

In winter I still feed three swims, but cup just one ball on a near line, three balls on a second line and one on the far line. On the second line, where I would expect to catch most of my fish, I usually cup three balls in leam or groundbait, which would be a mix of River International and Surface. But I would also put one cup of raw on that middle line. It doesn't really matter if it drifts down a bit, because I know that I've got three balls on the bottom and that raw ball can pull fish up the peg.

You need cups of differing sizes. I've got tiny ones for tough winter days, when I top up the far line with a thumbnail helping of joker, just enough to keep the fish interested. It's so light you don't even have to take it off, but can fish with it on the end of the pole. On the near bank I flick tiny helpings of perhaps 15 jokers held together by damp leam. It just holds together and you can flick it out about 5-6 metres. Boats can disturb your feed in winter, especially on your middle line, and you may have to put another ball in, or keep topping up with the tiny cup.

Bloodworm fishing can produce fish from 1 in (2.5 cm) long to 5 lb (2.25 kg). Although it's a deadly method, in the summer it can be a mistake to fish worm on the hook because there are so many little fish around. Though you seem to be catching all the time, those fish may weigh next to nothing. Then you have to switch to pinkie, which is a great summer bait, or to caster, big maggot or chopped worm. Putting in a load of joker isn't the answer, because it will just encourage more small fish.

When there are lots of small fish around, even changing to two or three bloodworm will not work. Tiny fish will still grab hold of one and worry it, so you have to keep changing your bait. You have to do some quick calculations when there are a lot of small fish in the peg. You may be catching half as fast on pinkie, but it may be bringing fish that are three times as large.

When conditions are hard, joker can be a killer bait. It's become an 'in' bait over the past couple of years, especially in Nationals where bloodworm has been banned. Double joker, fished 8-9 in (20-22.5 cm) off the bottom, particularly on nearside swims where you are flicking stuff in, can be very effective too on hard-fished waters.

Squatt fishing

Where bloodworm is banned, the main methods are punch, squatt or chopped-worm fishing. The squatt has really developed over the past couple of years. Floats are very similar to those for bloodworm fishing: very light – perhaps 0.1 g – with a wire top and wire stem. I use a 24 hook, but prefer a Browning 370. It's a slightly stronger hook because a squatt doesn't damage easily. Hooklengths are 0.05 in the winter, 0.06 in the summer. You are aiming to fish just off the bottom and on the drop. If you are getting bites that you don't see, move your shots close to the hook, though I would start with spaced shots. It's a very simple method: feed a few squatts, recast and do the same again, watching all the time for those bites.

Squatts are a brilliant roach bait. The only problem is loosefeeding them at distance and keeping them concentrated. I use a converted canal-type catapult with very soft elastic. Even if you pull it right back, it will only fire the squatts a certain distance. This concentrates them by giving the squatts a lob rather than a spread. If you need to use groundbait, perhaps because there's a headwind or you want to create a cloud, use sloppy stuff and add squatts to it. A wet ball can easily be thrown 12 yd (m). For groundbait, I use Van den Eynde Surface, which is a little sticky, gives a nice cloud but has no real feed value.

I prefer just a white squatt rather than a coloured one, and size is important. Try to buy big squatts, not so much for hookbait but for catapulting. They will go further. I clean them off but keep them in a little foundry sand. Don't put them in maize because it makes them float, and then you get every duck on the canal in your peg! The main thing about feeding squatt is to do so regularly. You only need to put in a few but feed so that there are a couple dropping through the water all the time.

Funnily enough, fishing a pinkie on the hook rarely gets you bonus fish when using the squatt. They seem to get preoccupied with the tiny maggot. Because it's such a light, weak maggot, it's worth trying the bottom of your peg, especially on a water with some tow, to see if there are bigger fish sitting there to pick up squatts that drift further.

Fishing the bread punch

Punch fishing requires slightly different tackle to bloodworm fishing because the bread has some weight when it's soaked in water. You can see its weight react on the float's bristle. I use a cane or nylon bristle, which is more buoyant, rather than wire. Punch fishes best when a canal is clear. The more colour you have, the less well punch fishes. That's why it's generally a good winter bait. In the summer, squatts in groundbait may be a better approach. If you can catch on the punch in summer, you can be more aggressive because your target weight will be higher. You will probably catch on the drop with spaced shots. The float will generally be 0.2 or 0.3 g. At the start of a competition, you should be fishing the punch 1-2 in (2.5-5 cm) off the bottom. That is generally a standard starter, though you'll catch a few fish on the drop. You may get a few fish 6 in (15 cm) off bottom or you might have to lay on the deck towards the end of a match.

You need very little feed when fishing a canal with punched bread. That's why the best method to feed is by cupping it in. Aim to fish two lines: one at 5 or 6 metres, similar to the bloodworm swim, and another at 10 or 11 metres depending on the canal. You would probably cup a couple of small balls about the size of a golf ball on each line and work between the two.

You don't get many of these on the canal! Me with a small thornback skate.

The feed is liquidized bread, made from slices of very fresh bread. I usually buy a medium-sliced loaf and cut off the crusts. Put it through a liquidizer, then run it through a maggot riddle to get the bigger lumps out. Seal it in a bag after squeezing the air out, remembering that bread dries out very rapidly. Be careful how much you use, because it fills the fish up so quickly. You might take half a loaf with you, but you would very rarely use that much. When you cup it in, it will float then start to sink, disintegrating and spreading out as it does so. I carry a selection of five different-sized punches, and I experiment through the day to find the size they will take best. One of the things you can do when bites have slowed is to try a smaller punch – and sometimes even a larger one.

I use a Browning 354, silver, medium-shank hook for punch fishing. I like silver because it matches the bread. I would probably start with a 22 and the second-smallest punch size. Particularly in winter, you have to keep changing your punch size. Bread dries out very rapidly and you need to turn a slice over or change to a fresh one every so often. I keep the unused slices in a sealed plastic bag.

I like to feed squatts close to, but not necessarily on top of the punch feed. I would put it just beyond the cupped bread. It doesn't seem to affect the swim at all, and a change of bait may bring you bonus fish. Generally, you are not looking to put much more in after that initial feeding. If roach are taking reasonably well, you might put another one on the nearside. If it's fishing well, you might feed four or five balls altogether through the day.

On punch, you will normally catch straight away, but then they get more wary. That's the time to start chopping round punch sizes and alternating between one line and another. If you're catching on the far line, don't bring hooked fish through the nearside line, but keep them clear of it. I always strike to the left and pull them out of the way. This is quite easy to do on canals because you usually have obstructions behind you.

Although I mainly use standard sliced bread, on canals I prefer a thinner-sliced bread although I'll take medium-sliced, too. On rivers, I would take thin, medium and thick sliced. Thinner-sliced bread gives less compression on the punch and expands quicker. The thicker-sliced holds better on the hook – it's a bit more tacky, and stays on longer. Because canal fish are more finicky, the smaller baits work best. A thick slice on a medium punch swells up to an enormous size.

Punch is the classic bait for small roach of 1 oz (28 g) or so, and it's amazing how large a punch those little roach can take. And you can get big fish, too. It will bring decent roach, and I've caught chub on it. I finished third in a match on the Cam with just one fish, a 12 oz (340 g) chub on the punch. You rarely catch perch on it, but you get odd ones, usually when you lift it. And skimmers are very partial to punch. If they're around, a switch to pinkie will often bring a bonus fish.

Big fish

Carp and chub can win you a match, though they can be very frustrating when they won't take on heavy tackle, but keep busting you on the very light gear. Carp are the biggest problem. There is no room for them to run out so they run along instead. They also like to live where there are lots of obstructions, and they are particularly good at finding these.

The pole enables you to fish to a snag and wait for a fish to come out and take your bait. But to have any chance, you must use really heavy elastic set tight and through only one, or perhaps two, sections. You want to stop that fish before it can get going.

Where carp are tight into snags, you have to be very positive in hauling them away. It means using perhaps 6 lb (2.7 kg) line and hooks like Drennan Super Spades. Normal match hooks are out. If I'm using maggot, I would be on a 16 as a tiny hook doesn't go with thick elastic. If you can get the presentation right then I reckon you are better off using rod and line than using a pole.

Tench are the closest to carp, very aggressive and good at boring into snags. But tench are not as strong as carp. When you are fishing for tench, get them straight to the top as quickly as possible. As long as you have a fairly heavy hook and strong line, you can then tighten up your elastic and put it through fewer sections so they can't go anywhere. Tench love casters. If I'm fishing a tench canal, I would always take casters with me.

Canal chub seem to have got bigger over the past couple of years, or maybe it's because we can get at them better with longer poles. Chub are not as violent as carp. When fishing for chub I'd probably use the same elastic as for carp, but wouldn't have it tensioned up so much. If the area wasn't too snaggy, I might even use No. 5 elastic. With carp, I'm on No. 6, or perhaps No. 8 elastic. The choice of elastic will always depend on the hook and bait you are using. You can use thick elastic if the fish will accept a 16 with double caster. If you need to go down to a 22 to get bites, you should use No. 4 elastic to balance the tackle.

Pole fishing on rivers

It didn't take long for the potential of the pole on canals to be realized. But many anglers are only just starting to realize that the pole can be just as effective on rivers. On my local water, the Cam at Cambridge, everybody would have been fishing a waggler or stick float only about three years ago. Now everybody has a pole out. Technology has advanced to such an extent that I can now fish the far bank on most pegs.

Of course you couldn't do that on a bigger river like the Witham, but the Lincolnshire river is a good example of how a pole angler should approach a slow-moving river. There are two main methods, depending on whether bloodworm is allowed and whether you have to fish for eels. Let me say now that I haven't got that much experience of fishing for eels, because I have no local venues with the same head of them. But I very quickly learnt how to catch them, what size float to use, and whether to use a long distance, perhaps 2 ft (60 cm), between the bottom shot and the hook. Eels are a strange fish, and very hard to hook. They can drive you crackers because of all the bites you miss. Light feeding is the key to catching them.

Let's start by looking at a bloodworm rig. Because a river like the Witham has more flow and depth, the float size has to be increased. I would probably use 0.75 g, or even upwards of 1 g if there was some pace on the water. I always use tungsten olivettes because they are two-thirds the size of lead ones and non-corrosive. Lead olivettes turn white and horrible. Tungsten olivettes are not cheap, but they last forever. The only time you lose them is when you lose your rig, which is not very often.

At this stage it's perhaps worth mentioning what to do if you get caught on the bottom. I've seen anglers breaking their pole tips or even losing them in the water by doing the wrong thing. To swing your pole up in the air and strike away wildly is a waste of time and a recipe for disaster. There's only one thing to do if you're stuck fast. Make sure your pole sections are in tight, and pull the pole straight back until your elastic bottoms out. Get hold of the elastic and pull in a straight line until your tackle frees from the snag or the hooklength breaks.

But back to the Witham. If there's not too much flow, I always go for a float narrower at the top than the bottom because it clears the water easily and I can spot those on-the-drop bites. I like a pear-shaped float, or perhaps just a slim style, but nothing that is bulbous or round at the top.

In an 8 ft (2.8 m) peg, I would fish 0.6 or 0.8 g if there's a bit of wind. I always use an olivette, but you don't want all

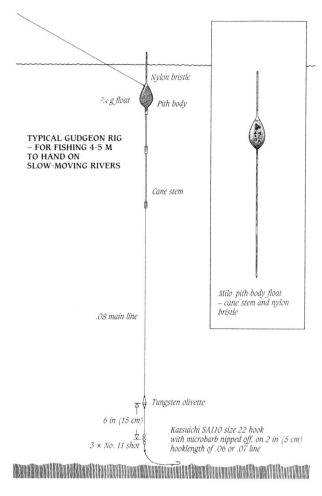

TYPICAL GUDGEON RIG – FOR FISHING 4-5 M TO HAND ON SLOW-MOVING RIVERS

Nylon bristle

³/₄ g float

Pith body

Cane stem

.08 main line

Milo pith-body float – cane stem and nylon bristle

Tungsten olivette

6 in (15 cm)

3 × No. 11 shot

Katsuichi SA110 size 22 hook with microbarb nipped off, on 2 in (5 cm) hooklength of .06 or .07 line

tungsten being sharp-edged, and you must have this silicone through the middle or your line will be damaged. I usually plug it with a nylon float bristle and trim this off exactly to length. With this, you can slide it up and down the line, make quick adjustments, and you never have to worry about damaging the line. The distance between olivette and hook depends on how fast the fish are coming. It could be as close as 10 in (25 cm) or it might go as far away as 2 ft (60 cm).

As a general rule, if you are fishing for skimmers, you want a hook that will take two or three bloodworm, with a little line on the bottom, and to put it through a bit slower. For roach, run it through off bottom with single bloodworm on a 22, although in summer, you can often get away with larger hooks. It's amazing how big a hook you can use with bloodworm, as long as it is fine wire and very light. Rivers like the Witham always seem to be prone to wind. I use a fairly long antenna to overcome this. The more chop, the slimmer the float, with most of the antenna submerged so you eliminate the chop but still spot those lift bites. Wherever you have flow, you will need more line between pole tip and float, and the harder it flows, the longer the line.

Feeding on a river like the Witham can mean putting in as many as a dozen balls, half of it joker and damp leam, but I use less surface feed than on canals. I use the Van den Eynde River Mix, which is designed for roach and skimmers when fishing with bloodworm. It's a reasonably heavy mix, but made less heavy by the amount of joker put in. At the start of a Witham match, I would probably feed 12 balls containing perhaps 750 g of joker. Remember, we are talking about a water with plenty of fish, and on harder waters you obviously need to cut back the feed accordingly. Don't forget to add the joker to the groundbait just before you feed.

On slow-moving water, I generally fish two lines: close in on the whip at 3 or 4 metres and at 12 or 13 metres. The farther line will be where the bottom starts to drop off and level out. It could be at 9 metres. But when I'm fishing for bream, I fish as long as I can. You have a better chance of catching the better bream at 14 metres, even if the drop-off is at 9 metres. My elastic will be No. 4 or No. 5 through two sections. In this situation you are using a bigger float, so you have to strike through it.

The punch is a brilliant bait right through the year, and on waters like the Cam and the old Nene, it is the prime method. The key thing with punch fishing is to feed all the time. I use 100 per cent white breadcrumb on rivers, but I

your weight in the olivette. I like to have five No. 11 or No. 12 shot as droppers, either spaced out or grouped three and two together for flexibility, depending on how the fish are feeding. When you are fishing to hand, it is a disadvantage to have too much shot spread. You want the bulk, and then just one or two droppers. However, with long pole, short line you haven't got to cast a float, so you can split the shots. You can have a smaller olivette and more droppers. You can always tuck shot under the olivette, but never either side of it. The shot above the olivette does nothing except stop the bulk from sliding freely up the line, and if you are catching a lot of fish, the bulk will be bouncing up and down and weakening the line.

Tungsten olivettes have a reasonable-sized hole in the middle with a piece of silicone sleeving through the middle. To fix them in place, you just cut this silicone about 1 mm overlength on either side. The machining process results in

don't bother to make it myself by liquidizing lots of loaves, I buy it in 56 lb (25.4 kg) bags. It's ordinary white crumb that has been dried and ground. I don't even bother to sieve it off before I use it because it's such good quality, but I prepare it the night before by wetting it. Add water very gradually and mix it as you go. It's better to underwet than overwet. Ten minutes later it has completely dried out, so you wet a little more. When it's the right consistency, run it through a maggot riddle to get out any lumps, seal it in a polythene bag and it's ready for the match. I usually take about 4 lb (1.8 kg) dry weight, which makes quite a bit more when it's mixed up.

With punch fishing, I usually feed just one line. If you can get them close, that's terrific and sometimes you can catch them at 3 metres to hand on the Cam. But I usually fish 6 or 7 metres, unshipping two sections. You need a bit of line to run down your peg and a float about 0.75 g. Although I use an olivette for punch fishing, it's positioned higher up the line than for bloodworm: perhaps 2 ft (60 cm) with three droppers. The lowest shot would be

about 10 in (25 cm) from the hook. My float, a nylon antenna, is always set virtually dead level to the water so I can see every lift bite, and fished just off the bottom.

Punch fish can easily drift down your peg, either because you are feeding too much or your feed is too light and needs squeezing a little harder. Even if you squeeze it really hard, it will still only go down a little bit before it opens up. It should never get to the bottom in one lump if you have mixed it properly. You can even throw it to the far bank and know it will dissolve as it goes down.

If the river is running hard, pinkies may fish better than crumb. Use normal groundbait or squeezed punch crumb hard, and fish pinkies on the hook so that you can hold back more. It's not easy holding back hard with punch.

When it's flowing, I always overshot my float. This forces you to run it through slower than the pace of the stream. The slower you want to put a float through, the more shot you add to it. If you get it right, you can hold the float dead still without it pulling out of the water at all. Bites are harder to hit, though. It might only be a tremble on the float. Somebody watching can't see it as a bite. In these circumstances, I try to keep my shot as near to the bottom as possible without actually being on the deck.

While I'm fishing a punch swim I try to keep a far bank swim going too. This may mean sacrificing a few missed bites while you feed regularly. But if you only feed when you remember, you will only have a few fish waiting when you go over. Keep regular feed going in, and you will often have fish lining up, especially some big roach, which often fall to a big maggot rather than a pinkie. It's hard work feeding two swims every cast, but if that is what it takes to win, that's what you have to do.

I rarely use groundbait on my far swim on the Cam because there, groundbait and big roach don't mix. In fact you don't catch any big roach on punch there now. They've wised up. I loosefeed pinkies, and only six or so every cast, using a special catapult with very soft elastic, which concentrates the feed. Sometimes the bigger roach just won't come up the peg and you have to fish a waggler to run right down for them.

One of the key things to remember if you're fishing a long pole is to leave something in reserve. If you start on your maximum line, say 14 metres, and the fish move out, there's nothing you can do. I'm lucky, being able to fish at 17 metres, but I certainly wouldn't ever start on that line. There comes a stage when it's better to switch to a waggler or even a slider on deep water. The essential thing is to present the bait properly. Don't go on the bank with a blinkered attitude, thinking that you always have to fish using the pole.

A classic example of this was in Northern Ireland when I drew end peg at Trory, an absolute dream draw, back in 1980. Everyone had been bagging up from it. I raced to the peg, dreaming of 200 lb (90 kg) catches. But it was an horrendous day with gale force winds and huge waves on the water. Only an idiot would have tried to fish a pole in those conditions – but that's just what I did, and to make it worse, I tried to fish it at 9 metres! I weighed in about 15 lb (6.8 kg) when I should have had 100 lb (45 kg), even in those conditions. I should have set up a feeder and just thrown it out. There were a ton of fish there, massive great hybrids, so I didn't need to go out very far. But I was blinkered: Ireland means pole fishing. That was in Ireland, but I see anglers do it here as well. They try to fish the far bank of a canal at 16 metres when there's a gale howling down the cut and the obvious thing to do is fish a waggler.

Pole fishing on stillwaters

I haven't talked about stillwater pole fishing yet. In the past few years, we've seen an explosion of quality lakes that offer excellent fishing from almost every peg. This almost becomes a problem in itself, because you run the risk of trying to cover too many methods and not doing any of them properly. Unless I am certain of doing well on a

Left: Catching on the Cam at Cambridge; a perfect water for the punch.

Right: Small carp – I love 'em! And they represent the future for many stillwaters.

feeder line, I will feed but use it only as a desperation measure. It just adds a further complication. I aim to feed two lines where I can catch steadily - playing the percentages. I know that with my approach I will figure in the money more often than not. The feeder may give me some wins, but it will give me a lot of blow-outs too. And anyway, I never think it's as much fun as watching that float go down. On the pole, I feel as if I am in charge of my own destiny if I work hard.

In the 1992 UK Championships, I had 35 lb 12 oz (16.2 kg) of perch and was beaten by 35 lb 15 oz (16.3 kg) of feeder carp. I don't see that as a defeat because it was so close that I could have won it, and I know who had the more enjoyable day's fishing. I never lose sight of the fact that I'm there to catch fish and enjoy myself. I'm not doing it for the money or the fame. If the fun went out of it, if I stopped enjoying catching fish, I would give up even if I was winning every match.

Even though the new, heavily-stocked waters give the feeder angler a chance to get very big carp, I'm confident that steady catching on the pole will be the right method most of the time. However, I always adapt my tackle for my target weight. If you are looking for 30 lb (13.6 kg), you've got to increase the elastic, and the hook and line size because you must fish far more aggressively. You can catch 15 lb (6.8 kg) of 2-4 oz (56-115 g) perch with a No. 2 or No. 3 elastic and 24 hook, but you can't catch 30 lb (13.6 kg) doing that.

Even if I'm looking for 10 lb (4.5 kg), I will still feed stillwaters reasonably aggressively. Ten pounds (4.5 kg) is a lot of fish. If bloodworm is allowed, I always start by putting some jokers in. However, I would probably not use bloodworm on the hook. In summer you risk being 'bitted out', so I would fish maggot or caster on the hook. But bloodworm and joker stimulate the fishes' interest and gets them feeding. If worm is not allowed, I would probably use groundbait with a few pinkies.

If I'm planning to use caster on the hook, I use Van den Eynde Hi Pro Specimen, a big-fish groundbait, for lake fishing. It has a few larger lumps in it to attract bigger fish. Even though you are catching roach, you are always looking to catch a few tench and carp. So a few balls of this would go in at the start, with casters in it. I would probably then loosefeed and see how the fish are responding. If I am catching on the drop and on the bottom, I would continue the loosefeed, but if there is no pattern to it, a small ball of groundbait with casters in every five minutes will often concentrate the fish.

A lot of people worry about the undertow on lakes. I love it. When there's a good tow on the water, that's usually far better for the fish. It's going to carry your bait a little way, especially if you are putting joker in, but if you are just loosefeeding caster, it's not a problem. It's easy to be deceived by the tow because the surface drift may be in the opposite direction. If you see your float going back against the wind, you know you've picked up the tow. If it goes the other way, you should be asking whether your line is too heavy. Is the wind pushing your float backwards when it should be going forwards? High-technology lines are much easier to control in this situation. A strong wind will pick up 2 lb (1 kg) Maxima, whereas it will not affect a 0.07 high performance line anything like as much.

Obviously the heavier the float and the more weight there is down the line, the more likely you are to pick up any undertow and run the float through properly. A float that's too light won't run through in the right way. So the lesson is: for reasonably deep water, you might need a slightly heavier float, even up to 1.5 g if there's a gale blowing. I would use an olivette on heavier rigs, but for standard lake fishing in 6-7 ft (1.8-2.45 m) of water, I like to space the shot, and fish as light as possible.

Pole fishing on fast-flowing rivers
The idea of using a pole on fast-flowing rivers like the Trent and Severn would have seemed ridiculous 10 years ago. Now it's the first thing many people set up. I love fishing fast-flowing waters on the pole, particularly as I have done well in several World Championships on waters that really couldn't be fished in any other way.

Flowing rivers call for a round-bodied float, perhaps a little bit on the oval side, but with the top of the float being the most buoyant part. With a round shape, you get equal pressure against the float and it holds down rather than riding up out of the water. The bad news is that it's the worst shape for striking. When you strike, you are pulling the float against the flow. You can't help doing this. There has to be a slight compromise, and that's why the oval shape has become popular. The perfect shape for flowing water is round, but it is far from ideal when it comes to clearing the water and hitting bites. An oval float comes out of the water a little bit more cleanly. Again, the speed of the stream dictates what you can use. On a really hard-flowing water where you want to hold the bait still or edge it down very slowly, you want a round float.

Once again, the rest of the tackle is increased in proportion. The elastics to use are No. 6 and No. 8 through three

Another roach to bronze maggot. On the Trent they must think it's a natural food.

sections. Often you will strike, and 4 ft of elastic will come out, even if you haven't got a fish. You've got to strike through the float, not at it. It's all a matter of using balanced tackle, so on a big, flowing river, you might need No. 4 droppers rather than No. 13s.

Bait will probably be maggot, so the hook should be 16 or 18 tied to 0.08. You can even go heavier if there are a lot of chub around. If there is some colour you can often push up your breaking strains to 0.10, and the main line to 0.14, or even 0.16.

Loosefeed is always best if the flow allows it. You must consider, though, whether you can still reach the fish. With a stick float, you can search right down the peg. You have to work out where the bait is dropping in the flow and whether it's going past your effective fishing area. Though the pole can be a great method on running water, it may-not always be the right one. On shallow, fast-flowing rivers like the upper Trent, you still need to consider the stick float as the first line of attack.

We have very few waters in the UK like the one in Yugoslavia that gave me my first World Championship win. There, the river was 18 ft (5.5 m) deep and flowing hard. There may be pegs on some UK rivers like this, but the fish rarely live in such swims in numbers. In Yugoslavia, with legering banned, no other method was possible except a very heavy float on the pole, heavy groundbait and the tackle held back hard. I think a scaled-down version of

this will become effective on rivers like the Trent over the next few years, in pegs where anglers have traditionally relied on the wand. I think the overshotted float, inched down a flowing peg, will bring surprising results for those willing to experiment.

Long pole, long line

The only other pole method I haven't covered is long pole, long line. Although the Italians have used this for years, the British only discovered its potential in Northern Ireland, where it was developed by Ian Heaps in particular. What's happened in Ireland is that we have had to fish farther out as the huge shoals of roach have disappeared. Don't get me wrong: there are still far more fish there than you catch in England, but they aren't around in the numbers they used to be. The result is that the norm now is 10-11 m. But it demands a different approach, even a different pole, to the one you use for long pole, short line.

The pole is used without any elastic for fishing a long line to hand, and you generally use it when you are getting fairly quick bites, not having to wait too long for the float to go. You don't have as much control, but the heavier float means that casting is not as much of a problem, and by mending to a heavier float, you are not automatically pulling it out of position. Irish fishing generally requires a float of 4-10 g, where you're fishing fairly deep water and looking to get your bait to the fish as quickly as possible.

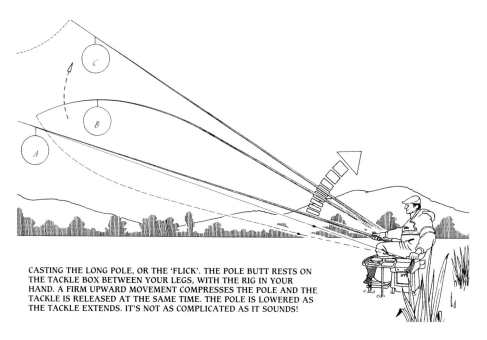

CASTING THE LONG POLE, OR THE 'FLICK'. THE POLE BUTT RESTS ON THE TACKLE BOX BETWEEN YOUR LEGS, WITH THE RIG IN YOUR HAND. A FIRM UPWARD MOVEMENT COMPRESSES THE POLE AND THE TACKLE IS RELEASED AT THE SAME TIME. THE POLE IS LOWERED AS THE TACKLE EXTENDS. IT'S NOT AS COMPLICATED AS IT SOUNDS!

The key thing for long pole, long line fishing is that you can't use your standard pole. It was not designed for fishing to hand, where the pole needs to be cast. The Italians in particular have developed some superb telescopic poles that are incredibly light but very flexible. Before we showed the potential of elastic, they always fished with flick tips and landed some very big fish on them. If you hook a 2 lb (900 g) chub on 4 m you'd probably lose it, but if you hook it on 11 m to hand, you'll probably get it in. Telescopic poles are nearly always used for this style of fishing, and you need to learn a special technique to get the float out.

The pole starts between your legs and on your box, which acts as a fulcrum. The cast is made by releasing the bait. As you do so, you flick the pole with the same sort of motion as when casting a stick float. You use the flexibility of the pole to catapult the float out. Irish fishing is easier because of the heavier floats required, which help the catapult effect. However, this sort of treatment puts an enormous strain on a pole – it's a very good way of breaking even the best stiff poles.

You need a pole with a bit of 'give'. It's possible to get a put-in pole that will handle this sort of fishing and short lining, but all the poles I use in this country for fishing to hand are telescopic, and I cut the tips back so I can land 2-3 oz (56-85 g) fish without having to net them.

I mentioned earlier that long pole, long line is fished without elastic, and the line tied directly to the pole end.

This method is for use when you expect a lot of fish, perhaps 300 in a session, because you can't cast if you use elastic, and you can't swing in 8 oz (225 g) fish. If you hook a bigger fish, say a bream, the flexibility of the pole and the heavy tackle soon beat it.

One of the few places in England where long pole, long line works well is on the Riverside Road stretch of the Wensum in Norfolk, though I think the Trent offers great scope for this method. Riverside Road is a unique place because you are sitting on concrete 4-5 ft (1.2-1.5 m) above the water. It is ideal for casting because you can let the line go and it doesn't drop into the water. The Wensum here flows quite hard and is 8-10 ft (2.45-3 m) deep and the fish are generally a fair way out.

You could fish long pole, short line there, but you are looking for 20 lb (9 kg) and that could be 200 fish, so you have got to be quite quick. On a long pole you would have to fish 15 m to reach the fish. A 10 m pole to hand is much faster. The float is controlled by the flow, and when you get bites, the fish is straight into your hand, unhooked, and the bait's out again. Even the fastest long-pole angler in the world couldn't match that.

Sometimes the fish will come closer, but I find with any kind of match fishing that the closer you fish, the harder it is to get bites. Fish beyond other anglers whenever you can, especially on a river. If you are the only one feeding on that line, you'll probably draw the fish of anglers below you as well, whereas they will be competing for fish.

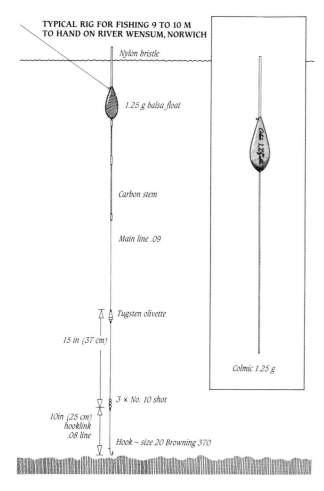

TYPICAL RIG FOR FISHING 9 TO 10 M
TO HAND ON RIVER WENSUM, NORWICH

Nylon bristle

1.25 g balsa float

Carbon stem

Main line .09

Tugsten olivette

15 in (37 cm)

Colmic 1.25 g

3 × No. 10 shot

10in (25 cm)
hooklink
.08 line

Hook – size 20 Browning 370

quickly. I usually change or paint the tips for this style of fishing, because most commercial floats have too fine a tip or the colour isn't right.

We are likely to see an explosion in the use of Bolognese-style fishing (see pages 142-144) over the next few years, and inevitably people will use this where they should be using long pole, long line. The Bolognese is designed for distance work, and there's no way you can cast a 1 g float on a Bolognese rig.

PREPARING FOR THE 1992 UK CHAMPIONSHIPS

The Whitbread, or MacPhersons, is now the UK Championships. I finished fourth in 1992, and it's still the hardest series to win because the competition is so fierce and the venues are so different. It's also a good illustration of how I prepare for matches on different waters.

Three ounces off winning at Willow Park

I was lucky because the first match in 1992 was on Willow Park, my home water. I didn't go down to practise for this competition specifically because I know it so well, but I always do a lot of preparation at home before any match. I'm often up until early in the morning tying new rigs, hooks and other little bits. I want to be prepared for every competition so that I'm never caught out by circumstances.

Summer at Willow Park requires a fairly aggressive approach, so I had to change my elastics because I was looking for weights of between 20 and 40 lb (9-18 kg). I have two heavy set-ups that I keep rigged up more or less permanently: a No. 8 elastic and a No. 6, both through three sections. I have six tips for my main pole, which should normally cover every possible situation. As the chart on page 81 shows, however, there are so many permutations. You can't be lazy if you want to win consistently. You've got to know that you'll have it absolutely right on the day. This means that you need a lot of extra tackle at home. It's no good realizing what you need at 7 pm when all the tackle shops are closed.

Wherever I'm going, I nearly always tie one or two new rigs the night before. Although I always carry around 100 with me, I like to know that I have a set-up that is spot-on for that particular water. I don't keep lots of spare rigs at home. I tie them as I need them, but much of the time I'm breaking down a rig that I used perhaps a couple of months ago and adapting it; otherwise, after a couple of months, I would probably find that I would need a tackle box just to carry my winders!

In this country I use 0.09 or 0.10 line because of the fairly heavy float needed, perhaps 1.25 g, and keep droppers to a minimum. Because you are casting rather than just positioning the float, spaced shots are a recipe for tangles. I usually have a hook length of 10-12 in (25-30 cm), then perhaps two No. 10s, often together, and the olivette 12-14 in (30-35 cm) above that. The vital thing is that the distance between your olivette and shot must always be farther than from your hook to your shot, otherwise you are sure to get tangles.

Never fish overshotted with this method, because you have little or no control over the float. As soon as you start to hang on a float that is farther out than the end of your pole tip in flowing water, it will be pulled towards you. You can control it slightly, but you need the wind just right to do so. I always use a pear or oval-shaped float, something that will come out of the water cleanly and

I don't date my winders, I just make a note of the float's weight, the line strength and type of line, and what length pole it is for on a piece of sticky paper, attaching it to the side of the winder. A typical winder would say: 7 m, 0.6 g, 0.7 Tectan. You can leave them in your box for a year. As long as they are out of direct sunlight, they will be in useable condition. If I take a float tray out in the sun, I'll lay something over the top. The other big factor affecting how long a rig will last is the frequency with which it is used. I break down a rig that has been used regularly after a month and set it up again because I don't want to take any chances with abrasion. A lost fish can mean a lost match.

Even tying new rigs takes more than just a few minutes. I usually know exactly what hook I want, and I'll tie several spares to the same hooklength, plus a few to heavier or lighter line. I know roughly what main line I'm going to use, but I always put it on over-length. When you get to your peg, you don't always know whether it will be 5 ft or 10 ft (1.5-3m) deep, and the last thing you want is to be tying rigs on the bank. I judge it by the length of the winder. A 6 in (15 cm) winder with 24 turns on it means 12 ft (3.65 m) of line. That will cover me for a 9 ft (2.75 m) deep peg, and if it's shallower I can easily shorten up. That said, I don't hesitate to add line if I need to. There is no need to worry about this so long as you tie the right knot.

I always take a while getting my floats set up exactly right. I use a spaghetti jar full of water and very slightly undershot the floats. All floats absorb a little water and they take a minute or two to settle down. You only discover exactly how long once you start fishing with one. I leave a float in the water to settle down, or rub on a little washing-up liquid to take off any grease from my fingers. I aim to have that float absolutely perfect from the very first cast. I don't want to waste even a couple of minutes adding styls or shot.

I always have plenty of hooklengths. You should never have to tie hooks on the bank. If I do need to, it means that I've already lost a dozen. I use small, easy-seal envelopes, available from any stationers, to protect them from the sun, and mark on them the hook model and the line it's tied to. I always mark the line by diameter, not by breaking strain, though I'll put on the make so I know if it's pre-stretched or not. I see a lot of anglers with their prepared hook traces on card or cork, which is all right if you keep them out of the sun.

At Willow Park, I know that I'm going mainly for carp. That means using a 0.09 hooklength, of about 1¾ lb (0.75 kg). I will probably use either Browning or Tectan –

both high-performance lines. These have a very fine diameter for their strength. The equivalent Bayer would have a breaking strain of about 1 lb (450 g). I'm a firm believer in high-tech lines on the pole because their reduced diameter cuts down the effect of wind on the line. You also have to remember that the elastic acts as a stretch, whereas with rod and line you haven't got that buffer so you have to use a line with some 'give'. Pre-stretched lines allow you to use a smaller float, and the extra finesse gives improved presentation.

Don't make the mistake of using high-tech lines on your reel. There is absolutely no give in them, and they break very easily because they're not particularly abrasion-resistant. For a reel line, I use Maxima if I want a very robust, sinking line. For a floating line I'll use Browning or Bayer Drennan Floatfish. You can always alter the line by quickly spraying furniture polish on to the line on the bank, but sprays are bound to cause line deterioration. Washing-up liquid is terrific for creating a very fast sinking line, but once again remember to renew your lines regularly.

I like round-bend hooks. I had an interesting meeting with some Japanese hook manufacturers recently, and they told me that round-bend hooks were just as strong as crystal. I also learnt that if one hook has nickel-silver plating and another is bronzed, the nickel-silver is slightly stronger even though the wire is the same. For the Willow Park match, I used a size 17 Browning 354, a round-bend, nickel hook, for its extra strength. It is a big hook, and just right for a single caster. In case it didn't fish well, I also made sure I had a bloodworm rig and hooks for that ready – tied as well. The caster rig might win me the match, but the bloodworm rig might still win me the section from an average peg.

I vary my hooklengths depending on where I'm fishing and what I'm after. My hooklength might be 2 in (5 cm) or 2 ft (60cm). I don't like using shot on the hooklength because if anything's going to go, it will be that. If you have shot on it, you have to go through the whole business of re-rigging to get it just right again. Wire-stem floats, in particular, are so tricky to rig just right.

For caster fishing at Willow, I like to use a dozen No. 12 shot equally spaced on the line, with perhaps a couple of No. 13s nearer the hook. I sometimes use shots as small as No. 15, but not for carp fishing.

I always check the weather forecast before any match, both on the night before and first thing in the morning. I think this is critical for any matchman because then you know what to expect. A heavy frost will call for a different

Sometimes even a sinking line won't cut through the surface film fast enough. Applying detergent to the reel line will sort out that problem.

approach; so will very strong winds, blazing sunshine and flat calm. On this particular day, the forecast was mild with quite a strong westerly wind.

Anything coming in from the west or south-west is going to improve fishing a great deal. So if you're fishing a river, it might add a bit of colour. On lakes, a southerly or south-westerly wind usually means good fishing. Information like this allows me to step up the feeding tempo, and even to go to slightly heavier rigs with confidence. On a canal, it might mean that I'm looking for 3 lb (1.35 kg) rather than 1 lb (450 g). A heavy frost, on the other hand,

may mean that I drop my target weight down to 6 oz (170 g). I usually associate high pressure with less good fishing, except sometimes in the summer months.

The other thing that I do before every match is to riddle my bait. Many people are astonished to find that I don't have a bait farm at my disposal, or the pick of a tackle-dealer's bait stock. I just buy my maggots, pinkies, red-worm and so on like everyone else. All I do before a match is to riddle off the maggots, put fine maize meal in with them and put them in the fridge. I never bother to put additives with my maggots.

Left: The catch that put me on the road to a unique double: my first day's net from the 1991 World Championships.

Right: Junior England international, William Raison, gets some inside knowledge on my groundbaits at Willow Park.

Many people think my success is down to some secret ingredient in my bait. I've seen anglers sniffing it after a match to try and discover what I've done to it. But with maggots and casters, I don't do anything. I don't believe in additives. The only thing I add is turmeric if I'm fishing bronze maggot. Otherwise it's just clean bait. I normally chill my maggots in the fridge, particularly in summer. Sometimes I'll chill them right down. They have to be very cold when you do this, and scarcely moving. Put them in a polythene bag, squeeze the air out, and tie the top. Then put them in the fridge. They stay in that suspended state until you go fishing the next day, and will be that much fresher. If you are going on a carp match, one or two will float naturally because they are really fresh and haven't worked any of the grease off.

I want casters to be as fresh as possible, ideally taken off on match morning. I just leave the bags open so they brown up a little. I like mixed colours of caster, and prefer them light rather than dark. For this match, I had 4 pt of casters and 1 pt (500 ml) of red maggots.

As far as tackle is concerned, the only other adjustment I might make is to check the elastics on my poles. I know that it's possible to rethread an elastic on the bank if the worst happens, but it's time-consuming. I always check them and replace any that show signs of wear. I replace fine elastics every month or two, but thicker elastics will last several months. Pole joints don't cause as many problems nowadays, but I use a joint-save that acts like a seal and extends the life of a pole significantly. To save myself problems later, I always wipe my pole with a towel when I'm packing up.

The only other thing I need is some groundbait, in case I want to put a feeder up. In summer bloodworm and joker are banned, and there are a lot of shallow pegs where you don't need them. But I don't want to be caught out. I carry some brown crumb and a bag of Van den Eynde Specimen. Sometimes you may need to put groundbait in with caster – when roach come right to the top and you can't get anything down to the bigger fish. If you try to catch those surface-feeding roach, you seem to miss every bite. I know some anglers mix their groundbait the night before, but I never bother except when I'm fishing bread punch.

I still get excited before a match, even after all these years. I often find it hard to sleep, especially when I know I will be on a lot of fish. I usually get to bed around 11 pm, but I'll never go to bed until I am satisfied that absolutely everything is prepared.

I don't have any real superstitions about the draw nowadays: drawing with my left hand, waiting until everyone else has drawn, wearing my hat backwards, that sort of thing. I used to like drawing late, but now I seem to have so much setting-up to do that I've got rid of that idea! I don't really have any superstitions while I'm fishing, either. I know some people won't pull their net out of the water, but I always pull it out to see what I've caught. I suppose the only superstition I have is to wear the white cap that has become very much my trademark. I bought my first one about eight years ago. I've worn all sorts of caps, but I saw this light-coloured one and liked it. I don't want to be aware of anything on my head, and sometimes when I'm driving home I can't remember whether it's on my head. They have to be washed very carefully by hand, but still eventually lose all their colour and get shabby. Then it's time for another one.

On this particular day I wasn't too bothered where I drew. There are fish everywhere on the lake in summer, and though the shallower pegs had been fishing well, I was looking for one about 5-6 ft (1.5-1.8 m) deep. I drew peg 92 on the willows, which is about 6ft (1.8 m) deep, so I was fairly happy. I knew there were a few fish in the area, though I hadn't fished this peg before. I had a tree to my left, and in front of me was just open water.

The first thing I do is to put the keepnet and box in position. I don't want to disturb the water any more than I have to, so I always use a stand, and I like to get down to water level. When netting big fish, you need to be as far out as possible. The water at Willow is always a bit coloured, partly because there are so many fish there, stirring it up and feeding.

I plummeted and found that it started to shelve off within 2 metres. After that the bottom was fairly level. I was looking to fish two lines: at 10 metres for roach, and closer in for perch and perhaps bonus carp. Of course I have the poles to go as far out as 17 metres, but there's no point here. The depth doesn't change and the farther out you go, the longer it takes to get fish in. I was expecting a lot of fish. My close-in swim was to be fished on a 7 m pole, but probably only 3 metres from the bank. I could flick casters there easily with my left hand.

My four rigs were light. I set up one ultra-light rig with a 0.1 g float for fishing up in the water; a maggot rig with 0.3 g float for fishing the deeper water, and two identical 0.2 g rigs. The float for the latter rigs had a fairly thick nylon bristle and cane stem, rather than wire, because I was using caster and fishing 10 in overdepth. Hook length was 0.09 to a size 17 Browning 354 hook. I'd set up two rigs like this, but the second was there only as a back-up. Many anglers might think these rigs were too light, but there wasn't much wind, it was only 6 ft deep, and with caster I expected to be catching on the last bit of the drop. I was looking for 15-20 lb (6.8-9 kg) of roach and perch.

Some anglers don't associate casters with perch, but big perch love them. I find perch prefer lighter, softer casters, whereas roach like the darker ones. If you are getting a lot of bites even with a biggish hook, hook the caster through the pointed end fairly deeply and bring the point back out so that it's lying inside the bend. It's quick and it still looks nice if they're having a go. Casters also allow me to fish a bigger hook and swing more fish.

I decided against setting up a feeder rod, though Tony Troth next to me had done so. Even so, I still seemed to be chasing about at the last minute and getting all my tackle positioned in the right place around me. You should never need to look for something during a match. If you bait up with your right hand, then your bait should be on that side. Swapping hands wastes time. I want my bait to be out of the water as little as possible. Though I am right-handed, I can throw with my left too. This is something I have worked at because there are occasions when it saves me time. When fishing a whip, for example, you never want to put the pole down. I unhook with my left hand, holding the pole in my right, even though I'm right-handed. All these little things add up during five hours. It can be as simple as not twisting round to get a disgorger or bending down to pick up groundbait. Everything should be within reach.

I'm always aware of what is happening either side of me, but I'm experienced enough not to worry if I get beaten. On this particular day, I could only see Tony on my right. He began on the pole, too.

At the start I loosefed casters. I was putting in half a pouch every cast for an hour, and flicking a dozen on the inside line. Within five minutes I was catching occasional roach up to 14 oz (395 g), perch of 2-3 oz (56-85 g), and I even had a tench of about 1 lb 8 oz (680 g). Tony was catching a few, but I was clearly ahead. It looked as if I was on course for my target weight. Then the better fish stopped feeding, and I could only catch small ones. I had tried the close-in line a couple of times and taken a couple of perch. Then decent roach started swirling, and I realized they were up in the water. To complicate things further, Tony had gone out on the feeder and had a 5 lb (2.125 kg) carp. That put him right up with me, and then he got another of the same size.

More than three hours of the match had gone and I started wondering whether I should change to the feeder. I decided instead to try for the big roach that were up in the water. I spent 15 minutes after them, and that lost me the match because I didn't get a fish. When I came in on the close-in line, the swim exploded.

Feeding time at Willow Park. Notice that I use a round bowl so that the groundbait is evenly mixed.

Shipping back with a fish on at Willow Park. A pole roller behind me makes this easy.

I went out and the float went straight away. Nice perch. I had about an hour like that and every time the float just went straight under. I have rarely caught fish as quickly. I must have taken 20 lb (9 kg) in the last 90 minutes. They weren't big, but I was catching them very quickly, and because of the No. 8 elastic I could swing them straight to hand. I stepped up the feed and put in a dozen casters every cast. The perch slowed up a little towards the end, but there were still quite a few there even when the whistle went. Tony had caught a couple more carp and he ended up getting one of about 7 lb (3.17 kg), so I presumed that he was way ahead of me.

I didn't think I had as much as I did, but I thought I should have enough for second in my section. I didn't realize I would get second in the match, and lose out by just 3 oz (85 g). Tony had 35 lb 15 oz (16.3 kg) and I had 35 lb 12 oz (16.2 kg). That 15 minutes spent missing bites from fish that were on the surface was an expensive mistake, though I suppose that if it had brought a big roach or two it would all have been worthwhile. I also lost a carp, but it was a double-figure fish and even with another 9 m of pole waiting behind me just in case a carp turned up, I had no chance. I expect to beat fish up to 7 lb (3.17 kg), but those double-figure fish are too big for the pole.

I always try to count my fish, which gives me a pretty good idea of the weight I've got, but at Willow I tend not to bother because the fish come in all different sizes and it's very hard to estimate their weight. That day I had more than 200 fish, nearly all perch. Just one more would probably have done it. There was a bookie at the match that day, so those few ounces cost me a lot of money. I won about £300, but it could have been a lot more. Still, in the UK Championships, section points are the most important thing, and first or second is a success.

A disaster on the Trent

After that great start, I had a terrible match in the second contest of the series, on the Trent at Long Higgin. I had only myself to blame for being too blinkered because I had come second in a match the night before, and assumed I would catch the same way. I had some excellent information on the state of the river from Wayne Swinscoe and Frank Barlow, while Kim Milsom, who's in the Van den Eynde team, had been practising. It looked as if I would be able to fish the long pole and catch plenty of fish on caster and hemp, changing to maggot if it got hard.

I had two rigs ready, one with No. 4 and another with No. 5 elastic. Because the Trent fish are a bit cute, I fished a size 22 Browning 380 hook to 0.06. There is not much pace on the Higgin in summer, and most of it is lovely pole water. I drew up to the left in the shallow field, where all the flow is on the other bank. I didn't really know that much about it, but it was a perfect depth, 6-7 ft (1.8-2.15 m) and just trickling through. I really fancied it for a few fish, especially as I won my first match on the Trent about three pegs away, weighing in 26 lb (11.8 kg) the very first time I had fished there with a pole. But my relative inexperience on running water showed because I should never have persevered with the pole. I didn't even set up a waggler or feeder because I was so convinced I would catch on the pole.

I had to fish quite long because that flow was on the other bank. I was using 15 m with a fair bit of line between float and tip so I could run down without the pole being directly over the fish. One thing about the Trent is that you can generally attack it because even if the fish aren't taking your feed, it's vanishing underneath the rocks on the bottom or being washed downstream. So I started by feeding half a pouch of hemp and caster every cast.

It soon became clear that it wasn't fishing very well. I switched to maggot after 15 minutes, and ended up fishing pinkie on the hook and feeding big maggots. A lot of people think you have to feed pinkie if you are fishing it on the hook, but it works just as well with big maggot, espe-

cially for carp. Soon I had cut my feeding right back and was only putting in half a dozen maggots. I was catching little roach, the occasional gudgeon and tiny skimmers, but every time I started to catch better it would die.

It was just one of those days when I read it completely wrong. The fish stayed more than a third of the way out, in the deeper water where it was about 12 ft (3.65 m). All the time I was thinking that they must start to feed soon. Everyone I could see was on the pole and I had a brilliant Trent angler, Keith Hobson, to my right.

Halfway through, Keith switched to a waggler, fished right across. He wasn't really catching much more than me so I didn't worry. But in the last 45 minutes he started to

It doesn't take many of these to make a weight. A good fish coming to net at Willow Park.

put some better roach together and finished with 8 lb (3.6 kg), beating me easily. I finished sixth in the section with 3 lb 9 oz (1.6 kg), and I was kicking myself afterwards for staying on a method that clearly wasn't producing results.

It was obvious halfway through that the fish weren't going to come, even at 15 m. I should have switched methods. And I shouldn't even have fished a waggler like Keith, because he's one of the best waggler anglers in the country and would probably have outfished me. I should have gone on the feeder two-thirds of the way across and just plodded away. I would probably have had 8-10 lb (3.6-4.5 kg), and a month later been £3,000 richer. Still, Kim Milsom, who knows the Trent far better than I, did the same as me and was last in his section.

I was annoyed because I let something get fixed in my mind. That's fine if you know a water really well, but I'm inexperienced on the Trent. I should have gone up and practised on the feeder. Afterwards I remembered having done the same at another match on the Trent – fishing a pole and not catching, then getting them on the feeder. It seems so obvious now – on a running water you will nearly always catch on the flow. I was deceived into thinking that I must be doing it right because experienced Trent anglers had poles set up as well. But that day the Barnsley lads took the first four places. They were all first or second in their section. They know the moods of the Trent and realized that the fish weren't going to feed on the pole line.

I have no doubt that there were 7-10 lb (3.15-4.5 kg) of fish willing to feed between me and the far bank. Because I was so confident that I could catch 10 lb (4.5 kg) on the pole, which would have put me first or second in the section, I'd totally discounted what can happen on the Trent. But it's difficult to calculate everything that can happen, and to cover every option. You can't have so many plans in your mind that you find yourself chopping from one to the other all day.

One of the things you have to learn when you've had a very bad result like that is to put it straight out of your mind. It would have been easy to lose heart, but when I analysed the results, it wasn't as bad as I thought. I was still lying seventh overall because almost everybody had suffered a disaster on the first match or the second. And though the third match on the Gloucester Canal meant a long drive – about 160 miles – I knew it fairly well.

Beaten by a lawn-mower

I went down the day before to practise and stayed overnight. This gave me the chance to get my rigs exactly right,

because this was going to be a bloodworm match requiring precise presentation. The practice session taught me quite a few little things and gave me confidence in my rigs. Though I practised on an average peg, I caught loads of fish, as you often do in practice. I always put fish straight back when I practise. I believe that retaining them in a net will make them unlikely to feed the next day, whereas they seem to have very short memories if you put them straight back. Perch are perhaps the best example of this. You can hook one and lose it, but 10 minutes later it will have another go.

The Gloucester Canal is a funny place because it shelves very steeply and careful plumbing is critical. You are looking for a tiny ledge. You may plumb and find a flat area, then it will drop away again. At 12 metres the water can be 15-16 ft (4.5-4.8 m), which is a bit deep to catch fish in the summer. So you aim to catch on 7-8 m. The ground rules are the same, summer or winter. Find a flat piece where your feed can actually stop, because on a canal with steep sides a ball of hard groundbait will just keep rolling. You have to use a groundbait that breaks up as soon as it hits bottom or just before, or make sure you can find a flat area for the feed to rest on, and feed a tiny bit short so it will roll down the side and hold.

My pole rigs for the Gloucester are all fairly similar, based on a standard olivette-type rig between 0.5 and 0.75 g. I've talked a lot about fishing very light and this rig might seem quite heavy compared to some I have been discussing. But the aim is to pick up what little tow there is. When the Gloucester flows, you catch fish, but if you haven't got weight down, you won't pick up that flow. If you use a very light float, it will go with the wind all too often, rather than the flow.

I set up three rigs, all 0.75 g, with two for bloodworm and another for maggot, to be fished a little further out. On the bloodworm tackles, I was using a size 24 fine wire SA10 Fly hook, which has a microbarb. A lot of the time I will fish barbless, which is best for hooking on bloodworm or joker because it doesn't damage the bait. But if you are using a really long pole and doing a lot of unshipping, you tend to get a bit of slack, no matter how hard you try. That's where the microbarb comes in. It might seem a very small hook for July, especially as it was tied to 0.06 line, but the Gloucester Canal fish are very crafty. In 1992 I caught 40 lb (18.15 kg) of big roach practising at Roundhay Lake in Leeds, where we won the *Angling Times*/Ruddles Winter League title. I took them all on a 24 hook. So you can still get big weights on a small hook.

I was using No. 3 elastic through two sections on the bloodworm rigs, and a No. 4 on the maggot rig. I expected my main attack to be on bloodworm. I had an excellent draw on the end peg. It wasn't the best area, but an end peg on a canal is always good. A few fish were topping, the water was warm, and I thought I would be on for a few. The bad news for me was that my team-mate Kim Milsom was in my section. He's the last person you want in your area on the Gloucester Canal because he's got such a tremendous record there.

I usually set my float up to about 9 ft (2.75 m) and then plumb up until I find that depth. So I decide the depth I want to fish first, then plumb around to see where that is. It was very steep close in, but then I discovered a little ledge about 7 metres out. It was only a plateau of 6-7 in (15-17.5 cm), but the key thing was that it was fairly level. I aimed to feed short of it, knowing my groundbait was going to roll that last little bit anyway. It was better than feeding right on to the ledge and taking a risk on missing it, which would take my fish away. And I fed very carefully, starting with only three little balls of groundbait and joker. My plan was to keep topping this up, because small balls don't roll so far.

I was expecting roach from ½ oz (15 g) up to 12 oz (340 g). After 10 minutes I started catching, and I was doing reasonably well when a mass of debris drifted along the canal towards me. Because I was the end peg, I was the first one to get it. It turned out that the lock keeper had

Who said matchmen only catch little roach? Here's a 1 lb-plus fish that would make anyone happy.

been mowing his lawn and chucked the grass into the canal. The bloody lot concentrated in my peg. I had to fish between tufts of grass for most of the match. I ended up fifth overall with 7 lb 5 oz (3.3 kg) and lost my section by 1 oz (28 g). I probably had more than 100 roach, the best being about 10 oz (283 g). There were plenty of fish there but I wasted a lot of casts because of the grass catching in my line. The match was only won with 8 lb (3.6 kg), so I could have won that one as well.

Nearly all my fish were caught on single bloodworm. I had just one roach on maggot. The only real change I made was to adjust the depth. Sometimes I fished just off bottom, sometimes just on, and occasionally I went out a little further with an extra section of pole. I used about 1 lb (450 g) of joker altogether, so it couldn't be called an expensive day's fishing.

Bloodworm fishing gets bad publicity and seems to attract a lot of bans because of occasional heavy feeding. People claim that heavy quantities make match fishing too expensive. And it's true that the 1991 Super Cup at Holme Pierrepont was easy to criticize because of the huge amounts of bait that were being used. But the fish were there to eat it. The water has a huge head of roach, and a lot of bream. If you threw in 12 balls loaded perhaps with 1 kg of joker, it was gone within an hour. There were just so many roach that you needed about 2 kg. I'll admit it's expensive, but that match was an exception. Bloodworm is a bait that brings bites when you wouldn't get them on anything else. And fishing is, after all, about catching fish.

That said, I think we sometimes feed too much. No one would chuck in 1 gal (4.5 litres) of maggot and then sit there for five hours fishing on it. The French get away with a heavy initial feeding because they are fishing two-hour matches, but in the English five-hour contests, you just can't often last that long without feeding again. I like to put some in and see how the fish respond before adding to it. It's more versatile that way.

Happy memories at Worsborough

The Gloucester Canal result pushed me up to fifth place overall, and the final match of the series was on Worsborough Reservoir at Barnsley, where I'd won the previous year with 65 lb (29.5 kg). It was one of the best match weights I'd ever had in England, and once again it came about as a result of practice. I had learnt that the fish were up in the water, and although I'd caught a few bream in practice, it was nothing like my experience on match

day. My peg, which was 15 ft (4.5 m) deep, was next to the one I had fished the day before. I had fed quite large balls of soft groundbait loaded with caster and squatts every cast, and fished it 3 ft (3.95 m) deep with a tiny 0.1 g float. I pulled a caster back into the feed and almost every cast I was getting bream of 2-3 lb (900 g-1.35 kg). That catch helped me to finish third in the 1991 series, and brought me nearly £4,000 because there was a bookie.

I wasn't expecting to repeat such a catch this time. The reservoir wasn't fishing as well and though conditions were reasonable, I drew in the shallows on the right-hand bank. It was only 3 ft (1 m) deep. Barnsley's Alan Scothorne, who was winning the league and who had won it the previous year, was two pegs from me.

As I had drawn a shallow peg, I knew I couldn't catch fish up in the water. It meant fishing caster on the bottom. But I still used a 0.2 g float with shot spaced down the line. I expected that I would be looking for better roach, so I planned to bury the caster. My elastic was No. 4, and my end tackle 0.08 hooklength to a size 18 Browning 354.

Having missed out at Long Higgin, I made sure not to repeat my mistake and set up a feeder rod. At the start, I put four balls about 30 metres out, a nice easy chuck. The way to fish the feeder there is to use only a tiny strip of thin lead, just enough to tighten up to, with a short tail to the feeder and a very short hooklength, because those skimmers hardly register a bite.

On the pole line, I fished 12.5 m with softish groundbait, a 50:50 mix of Surface Cloud and brown crumb. I wanted to throw a big handful and it's a job to throw a sloppy mix, so I used a dry crumb that just held together. I started to catch roach of 5-6 oz (140-170 g) on caster. I was doing quite well, putting in the occasional ball of groundbait, and wondering whether they were responding to it. Alan was doing the same and getting the odd fish, but not as many as me. I couldn't make out whether the groundbait was scaring the roach or whether it was worth continuing with to bring in the bream.

I knew from the previous year that you needed groundbait to catch bream. But were there any bream there or would I have to rely on catching 20 lb (9 kg) of roach? Then the roach slowed. I had 2-3 lb (900 g-1.35 kg), and was starting to struggle. After three hours, I wasn't sure what to do. Then the angler next to me made things even more complicated by putting in a hard ball of groundbait and getting a bream. It seemed to me that groundbait wasn't scaring them, even though it was only shallow, so I started to feed more aggressively. I switched from putting an odd ball in and loosefeeding to feeding heavier with groundbait and cutting back on loosefeed. It took a while to build up. Alan had meanwhile gone out on the feeder and was getting some skimmers. Then I started to catch on the pole, and in the last hour I had four 2 lb (900 g) fish.

I finished with 20 lb (9 kg). The first two pegs in my section were first and second in the match with 40 lb (18.15 kg) nets. I was third in my section and fifth in the match, which gave me fourth overall. I was unlucky that the top two in the match were in my section. Those two points would have given me second in the series, and if I had done half decently on the Trent, I would have won the series again.

That day I lost a couple of very big hybrids, which actually broke me. Hybrids fight very hard, but it takes a lot to break 0.06 line! At Worsborough, you'll catch hybrids early on or not at all. On the plus side, fishing very light had brought me roach when others hadn't been able to catch them.

OTHER MEMORABLE MATCHES

I've now won hundreds of matches. Several top anglers keep a note of all the matches, but all I do is to record my wins. A lot of the minor wins have disappeared into the back drawers of my memory. I've got such a bad memory that I only remember those that produced a very big weight, or were special for some other reason.

One that falls into this category is the King of Clubs. This is an Irish festival, and it started as a contest for club champions on three different styles of water. But with £3,000 top money, it soon became a magnet for top anglers and winning it is just as hard as the UK Championships. I won it in 1990, just three days after I came back from winning the World Championships in Yugoslavia.

Because it has become harder to find three different waters that will accommodate 150 anglers and still provide guaranteed good fishing, the event is now held just on lakes. It's decided on section points, so really you are fishing 25-peg matches each day, though obviously if there is a points tie, it is decided on weight. The venues were Killykeen, the opposite bank, called Eonish, and two smaller waters, Church Lake and Rossduff.

I had no time to practise or to do my usual preparation. It was complicated because of the post-World Championship media interest. When I got to the guest house where I stay every year with Kevin, the owners had put up big banners: Welcome Bob and Kevin. We had a champagne reception and all the local press were there. Then the BBC flew a camera crew out from England, which was unheard of for fishing.

I drew Killykeen on the opening day. It had not been fishing well. One end of the stretch is pole fishing because it's deep close in, another part is waggler because it's 3-4 ft (1-1.2 m) deep as far as you can chuck, and the far end, where I drew, is good night. There are hardly any bream there and few roach. It's 7 ft (2.15 m) deep and I knew that the only thing I could do was to fish a waggler and hope. I was fishing against pegs that nearly always produce well on the pole.

I set up a pole, more to pass the time before the match started, but my plan was to stay on the waggler and keep loosefeeding. I expected to use up to 3 pt (1.5 litres) of bronze maggots, but I wasn't expecting to catch many fish. I thought I would do well if I caught 5 lb (2.25 kg). To my enormous surprise, I won the section with 17 lb (7.7 kg).

People read about big Irish catches and assume you can catch the fish on meat-hooks. You may have been able to when it was relatively undiscovered, but a lot of the time now, you have to fish it with English tackle and tactics. That's just what I did, using a 20 hook and 1 lb (0.5 kg) bottom, and fishing a 3AAA waggler four rods out and over-depth, running it with the wind. The fish were mostly small roach, though I had a few little hybrids of about 6 oz (170 g) and a couple of perch. I didn't catch any big fish.

My section had fished quite well. Everybody had at least 3 lb (1.35 kg) and there was a 13 lb (5.9 kg) weight, but I was well clear, from an area that really should have been a no-hope one. I had some luck because the pegs at the other end of the section, which had the potential to produce 30 lb (13.6 kg) nets, didn't fish at all. But it was a time when everything was going right for me. It's the angling equivalent of the 'rub of the green'.

I was on Killykeen lake for the next match, but the opposite bank this time. It was low, warm and the main quarry was roach because there weren't many bream about. It demanded a very different approach to the previous match, because the lake was very calm and I knew those roach would not be in close. I used a 6 SSG waggler and fished about 40 metres out. Over the past two years, I have learnt a lot more about slider fishing and think that I would probably have done better on a slider. Because it was at least 15 ft (4.5 m), deeper than I had anticipated, I had trouble casting, even with a 14 ft (4.25 m) rod. Netting fish was difficult too.

I fed with balls of groundbait, which broke on impact. I put a few casters in, but it was mainly cloud. I was aiming to

In places such as Ireland and Denmark, it's often necessary to get well out into the water. You need not only waders but a suitable stand.

catch roach on the drop, using a 20 hook and 1 lb bottom again. The light approach worked well once more. I finished second in the section with 10 lb 5 oz (4.6 kg), beaten only by bream on the end peg.

With a first and a second, I was praying for Rossduff, because it was producing big weights of skimmers on the pole. I had been down there and practised the day before and bagged up. But it looked as if my luck had run out when I drew Church Lake. All I knew about it was that there were some roach on either end of the section; that odd big bream could be caught on the feeder, along with a few hybrids; and that it was fairly deep on the pole line.

My peg had a 14 ft (4.25 m) on a 13 m line, and it hadn't produced in earlier matches. With that depth, I didn't fancy it for roach. Because the bream were big fish, I realized that I only needed a few and I thought I would have as much chance on the pole as the feeder, though I realized that I would be very lucky if I got a winning weight on one line. So I fed a pole line and a feeder swim. I started on the pole, laying-on with double caster, and caught a couple of hybrids, then went out on the feeder. I kept swapping between the two, but ended up on the feeder, getting one decent bream near the end. Every time I caught a couple of fish and thought that they might start to feed well, the peg would die and I would have to rest that area and fish my other swim.

I weighed in 18 lb 6 oz (8.15 kg), which was a good weight for the peg, but it only gave me fifth in the section and I didn't expect eight points to get me anything except a minor place. But the angler who was ahead of me blew out completely, and all the others who were in with a chance did badly, too. Lady Luck was certainly with me that month! I won the £3,000 top prize, plus about £350 for section placings during the week.

That win came about as a result of taking a far more cautious approach than many people think is necessary in Ireland. But Irish fishing, both in the north and south, has changed enormously over the past decade, as I'll explain in the next chapter.

I love team fishing because I can battle away in a poor section and know that what I'm doing can make a big difference at the end of the day. It's also very satisfying to be part of one of the country's best teams, Van den Eynde Essex. This was put together in 1991 by my long-time friend Pete Clapperton, and the idea was to bring to angling the same professionalism as football. Peter, who's a visionary when it comes to fishing, believes that we will soon be seeing substantial fees changing hands to get the best anglers, and he pre-empted this by paying what in angling terms is very big money for stars like Kim Milsom, Wayne Swinscoe and Pete Vasey. The anglers in the team are also paid a salary to fish, and it's by far the best deal in angling so far.

Some have claimed that team fishing spoils the sport, but on the contrary, it has made it more professional, and seems a logical step. And to prove that you *can* buy success, we won the *Angling Times*/Ruddles Winter League in our first full season. The match was at Roundhay Park in Leeds in 1992, and I like to think that I am responsible for masterminding our win.

We had also won the southern semi-final on the Gloucester Canal. I hadn't fished because I was out of the country, but Kim Milsom, who knows the names of every fish in the water, got it absolutely right. The semi-final was a good match to win because there were some excellent bloodworm teams taking part, such as Dorking and Trev's Browning. Peter insisted that all our team had to go down there and practise. Those practice sessions warned us of what it would be like, because the fishing was completely diabolical. However, we learnt that it was absolutely vital to feed precisely.

The plan was to put some feed in, but to start by throwing a lead or small feeder to the other bank with a white maggot. There was a chance that one of the 12 might catch a chub. And it was a good tactic because there wasn't much happening on the inside for that first 30 minutes in any case.

The feeding on the inside was done by cupping, after finding out where there was a small shelf. It was generally around the 7 or 8 metre mark. Cupping the bait enabled us to be very precise, and all we put in was three balls of raw joker with just a little bit of leam. When you are aiming to catch 2 lb (900 g) of fish, you can take your time. You might spend 10 minutes cupping, but it's vital that the bait goes in the correct spot, because one ball in the wrong place means fish in the wrong place. It was a softly-softly method, designed for catching a fish. If they fed well, we could easily top up, but once you've put in a lot of feed, you can't take it out again. The method worked brilliantly. Everyone caught fish and we won the match.

Roundhay Park was a different proposition because we didn't know it well. It meant that we had to work hard to find out the way to fish it.

I discovered in practice that I could catch roach just as I had at Worsborough Reservoir in Barnsley, but using bloodworm and sloppy balls of groundbait with joker. A lot of Roundhay Park is 15 ft (4.5 m) and those roach don't want to be on the bottom in summer. By feeding groundbait and joker just 3 ft (1 m) deep, and fishing a 24 hook with single bloodworm, you could catch roach to more than 1 lb (450 g) – and lots of them. In practice sessions, I was getting up to 50 lb (22.7 kg).

When you start fishing, you do it all wrong by setting your float 2 ft (60 cm) deep in an 8 ft (2.45 m) peg. As you learn more, you start to fish on the bottom and it becomes ingrained in your mind that the fish are always on the bottom. But there are a lot of fish, particularly in summer months, which can be caught at a depth of 3-4 ft (1-1.2 m). Just think of those times when you've been swimming in a lake and hit a 'cold spot'. If you put your feet down, you can feel how much colder the water temperature is. Fish are like us; they prefer warmer water. There might not be so much food there, but that doesn't matter. They can go on to the bottom to feed. And if there happens to be food in these warmer areas, they will eat it. Simple, isn't it? I've fished 3 ft (1 m) deep in water of 10 ft (3 m) or deeper loads of times. It seems so obvious in summer, and I was astonished that no other team had worked it out.

If you discover something special, you always want to keep it quiet. We made a point of not fishing like this in practice too much, but a lot of our success was due to the fact that the other teams were so confident that they had the right method as well. For Barnsley and Goole, it was almost a local water.

Not all the pegs were deep, but the 4 ft (1.2 m) swims weren't a problem. It was the deep water that needed sorting out. Our method worked like a dream. Although we were fishing against the best teams in the country (we had Barnsley and Goole on either side of us), we won by a mile, thanks to our method in the deep pegs, where we won five of the seven sections and finished second in the other two.

Even though it didn't fish anything like as well as it had in practice (and it very rarely does) we still caught roach up in the water. It was a cold, wet day and the fish weren't feeding in quantity up in the water. But they didn't want to be down on the deck either. I drew on the deep water and I doubled everybody's weight in my section, catching 14 lb (6.35 kg) of roach for the best roach weight in the match. I had to change depths throughout the match, sometimes catching at 8 ft (2.45 m) deep, but I also got several bonus fish on redworm, which was another thing we had discovered in practice. That's where a runner is vital on a team match. When I started to catch on redworm, I told our runner and he conveyed this to the rest of the team. Two of the side shot right up their section as a result.

I was captain that day, but I'm not really much of a team captain. I'm too dedicated to fishing. I can't be bothered with phoning people here and there and playing mum. I've got no aspirations to become team captain or team manager, and I'm not a good administrator. If it was left to me, we would be turning up with half a team and no bait!

5

THE THINKING ANGLER

*I*f you want to win consistently, you can't just pick up your tackle from the weekend before and head off for a match. Competition is stiffer than ever before, so I look for anything to give me the slightest edge. That's why I always ensure that my tackle preparation is thorough and that I am covered for every eventuality. The result is one of the heaviest tackle boxes on the riverbank, but it means that I'm never going to be caught out by a shoal of feeding bream, a broken elastic or a snaggy swim that results in a lot of lost tackle. My tackle box has all I need for any match – and a lot more besides.

Who says I don't own a feeder rod? Catching roach on Ten Mile Bank.

MY TACKLE-BOX

I use an ASI box for all my fishing, rather than one of the lighter models that have come out over the past couple of years like the Boss and Conti boxes. It might not be the best for carrying, but it's certainly the best for pole fishing and it's so strong that you never need to buy a new one. One of my friends has had the same box for 10 years and it's as good as new. It's got a terrific capacity, and I can carry everything I need in it.

The topmost section, where most people put their floats, holds about 60 pole-winders. The pear-shaped floats are my favourites, and most have orange tips. If I need a black tip, I just paint it on the bank with a felt-tipped pen. Every winder is marked on the side with the main line, hook length and shotting. Every so often I put them in order, but when you're fishing a lot they're bound to get mixed up. Some of these rigs may stay in here for a year,

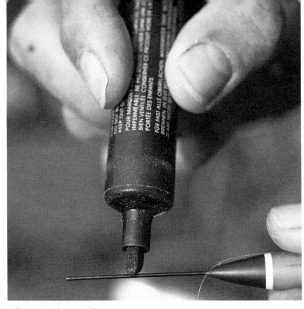

Above: The quick way to change your float colour when the light changes.

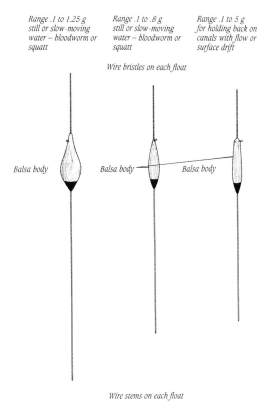

Range .1 to 1.25 g
still or slow-moving
water – bloodworm or
squatt

Range .1 to .8 g
still or slow-moving
water – bloodworm or
squatt

Range .1 to 5 g
for holding back on
canals with flow or
surface drift

Wire bristles on each float

Balsa body

Balsa body

Balsa body

Wire stems on each float

All this range hand-made by French float-maker

TOP FLOAT CHOICES FOR POLE FISHING

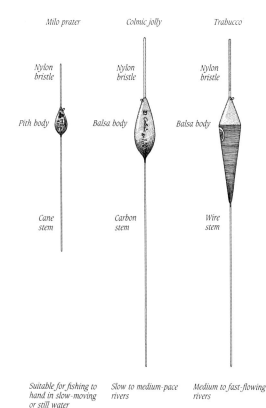

Milo prater

Colmic jolly

Trabucco

Nylon
bristle

Nylon
bristle

Nylon
bristle

Pith body

Balsa body

Balsa body

Cane
stem

Carbon
stem

Wire
stem

*Suitable for fishing to
hand in slow-moving
or still water*

*Slow to medium-pace
rivers*

*Medium to fast-flowing
rivers*

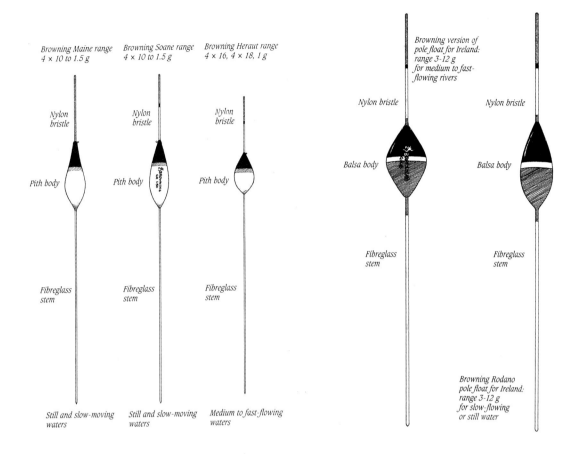

Browning Maine range
4 × 10 to 1.5 g

Browning Soane range
4 × 10 to 1.5 g

Browning Heraut range
4 × 16, 4 × 18, 1 g

Browning version of
pole float for Ireland:
range 3-12 g
for medium to fast-
flowing rivers

Nylon
bristle

Nylon
bristle

Nylon
bristle

Nylon bristle

Nylon bristle

Pith body

Pith body

Pith body

Balsa body

Balsa body

Fibreglass
stem

Fibreglass
stem

Fibreglass
stem

Fibreglass
stem

Fibreglass
stem

Still and slow-moving
waters

Still and slow-moving
waters

Medium to fast-flowing
waters

Browning Rodano
pole float for Ireland:
range 3-12 g
for slow-flowing
or still water

if I'm not using them much. I make up new rigs for each competition, so I'm probably tying another five each week. I take out the tattiest ones and strip them down, or I would need three ASI boxes to carry everything by the end of the season!

I have a workroom at home, but I don't store winders there, except the Irish ones, which are very specialized with heavy line and big floats. I take more than 100 to any match, which is enough to cover every situation, but it's important to do this in advance because you don't want to waste time doing it on the bank (see page 122). I also duplicate the rigs I am most likely to use because it's easy to get caught on the bottom or in a tree. All I have to do then is tie on the duplicate, which only takes about 30 seconds. All rigs have more line than I will need because I don't know the exact depth of the peg I'm going to be fishing and it's easy to shorten the line.

Most people who see my rigs are surprised that I use shop-bought floats. The quality of these is so good that it's a waste of time to make one's own. That said, every one of my floats has had something done to it. Most have been hand painted because there was not enough depth of colour for me. I put on a base white, then repaint them with an orange blaze, which is the easiest colour to see in most lights. I also add a black top to help me spot on-the-drop bites. That extra coat of paint also makes the bristle slightly thicker, which helps with visibility at long range. I always varnish nylon stems. Nylon bends, breaking paint, and varnish protects the stem. On some floats I put in longer wires, which increases their stability but cuts the amount of shot needed down the line. This way I can turn a 0.2 g float into a 0.1 g, and it will need only four tiny shot.

The second tray in the box carries another 40 winders, with some larger floats like sticks and wagglers already set

Packing up after a match at Willow Park. You can see how many made-up winders I carry.

up. The third tray carries most of my wagglers and some sliders. They are mainly peacock, and painted two-tone to spot lift bites. Again, I don't bother to make my own any more. The quality of peacock is so good and the finish so neat that it's not worth trying to do better. Most of these floats have shot, lead-free of course, already attached underneath to a small length of line. It means I know what I need, rather than wasting time adding a No. 4, finding it's too heavy, and changing to a No. 6. Some wagglers have tiny swivels attached to the bottom, others float-adaptors, so the float folds over when you strike and your strike is connecting with the fish and not being absorbed by the float.

The bottom tray carries my stick floats, mostly the Dick Clegg range, which are made of lignum. I don't use them just because he's the England team manager! Lignum is a very dense wood and when you hold back, the float does not ride out of the water. All my sticks carry three pieces of silicone tubing, rather than two, to stop the float slipping. The bottom piece of tubing protrudes slightly from the bottom of the float to help stability.

Another tray contains all the little float accessories, such as different thicknesses of silicone tubing. I suppose there are about 150 loose floats in it. I know that I carry more than I ever need, but what to leave out?

The first of the outer boxes carries hooklength lines. I have lots of Damyl Tectan, which I sometimes use for main line because it is stiff and tends not to tangle. I carry Tectan in the spools I use most: 0.07, 0.08 and 0.09. It is not quite as good for hooklengths. For that, I'll use Browning High Power or an Italian line, ProMicron. The lightest I carry is 0.05, which is 12 oz (340 g). It's pre-stretched, very fine and soft.

In the same compartment are my small pole pots. I carry several sizes, and make my own. The smallest is only 1 in (2.5 cm) in diameter, for feeding very small quantities of bait very accurately. I have larger ones as well, including those for initial cupping, which will take about ¼ pt (225 ml) of joker.

There is a shot container, carrying sizes from No. 8 to No. 13, and two containers of pole-elastic lubricant. I'm using this all the time, so I make sure that I never run out. My first task after setting up is to squirt some of this into the pole to ensure that the elastic runs smoothly. There is a drawer full of odds and ends: a small bottle of washing-up liquid for degreasing the line and to make it sink quickly; a pair of fine scissors for trimming knots; a container of instant-colour orange paint and a black marker pen for changing the tip colour of wagglers; and a spool of insulating tape. It's amazing how useful that is. I often tape my reel to my rod when I am catching a lot of fish to make sure it doesn't move.

Another drawer contains other bits and pieces: a pair of wire-cutters, mostly used for setting up olivettes, clipping off a piece of nylon bristle or a bit of wire from a float; a pair of styl pincers; a pair of scissors for chopping up worms; and a pair of long-nosed pliers. I use the latter mainly for pulling small bristles out of an olivette. I wouldn't be without a knot-remover. It has a very sharp end and when you are using light line, you get a lot of wind knots. It's a mystery how it happens, but with this you can pick them out. If you leave a knot in the line, you have a weak point and the start of further tangles. My set of bread punches are in use a lot. Although they are commercially made, they have been set into a plastic biro tube to make

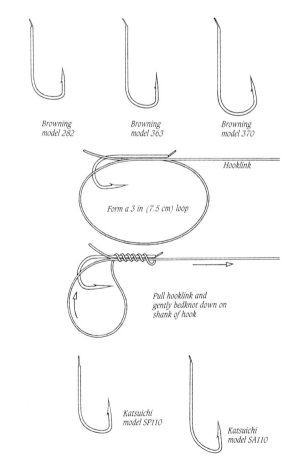

Browning model 282

Browning model 363

Browning model 370

Hooklink

Form a 3 in (7.5 cm) loop

Pull hooklink and gently bedknot down on shank of hook

Katsuichi model SP110

Katsuichi model SA110

HOOK-BEND PATTERNS AND SPADE-END KNOT

them easy to grip, and have a slit in the side for bringing out the hook. I think those without a slit can blunt a hook.

Candle-wax might seem an odd thing to carry, but it's very good for tightening a loose joint. Tweezers get used a lot when I'm bloodworm fishing, and want to pick out hookers. I use a grey tray with a light bottom so I can see the bloodworm, and fill it with about ¼ in (6 mm) of water. Water magnifies things, so when I sprinkle blood-worm into it, I can easily pick out the biggest for hookbait. It takes ages if you try to do it with your fingers.

The disgorger is a very interesting device that will sell like wildfire once it becomes easily available in this country. It was designed in Italy last year and I've never known a disgorger like it for getting hooks out of deeply-hooked fish, even eels. You don't even have to look to use it. Just slide it on your line and bang, the hook's out. I carry a knife-edge needle-file because it is the best tool for cutting carbon, particularly carbon tips. A hacksaw will tear the fibres, but with a knife-edge you can run round the tip of the pole and have it ready in seconds.

I have a selection of non-toxic bombs, a couple of plummets, some cable ties for catapults, and a hook wallet. This is bursting with pre-tied hooks of all sizes, from 14s to 24s. Everything is marked with the line type, the length of trace and the hook pattern.

I always carry a diamond-eye pole-threader in case something goes wrong with the elastic and I need to re-thread it. I don't usually carry elastics with me, so I am in trouble if I break elastic, but usually I have enough spares to get by. You never know when it might slip through, but I can re-thread it without much trouble.

A lot of people use fine plastic sleeves to attach their pole floats. I only use them on the end of flick tips. They are too stiff for floats and have no give at all. I always use silicone sleeves instead.

Some of my catapults are standard, like the whopper-dropper; others have my own adaptation for pole fishing to ensure a tight pattern of feed. One has very weak elastic so that it easily reaches its limit. If the wind is right, it will keep the bait in a foot-square area.

I use a spray bottle, the sort of thing you get in garden centres, to freshen up jokers and to dampen leam, which makes it bind together.

I find the V-type pole-roller better than the extended U-style, which can make your pole waggle all over the place. In addition, I think a pole on the V-type slides better. I don't use rests, apart from a front pole rest. If you are on a steep bank and shipping back, where do you put the pole? If it's on a roller, it will roll forward – and into the water. The front rest clips the pole in place and stops it rolling forward.

The only reel I use is the Browning 810. I've got four in the box. They have a big handle, are ultra smooth, hard-wearing, and the bale arm flicks over from any point. Another advantage is that when you're playing big fish such as carp, you can actually put on extra pressure with your

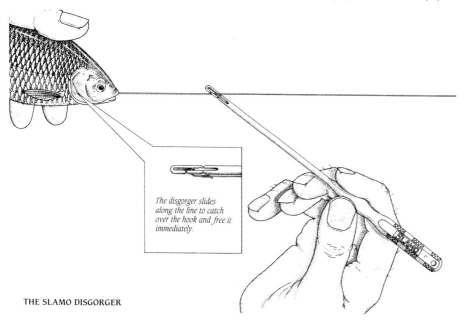

Right: Feeding with a catapult. Notice that the catapult is held sideways. This stops the elastic recoiling back and whacking your knuckles.

The disgorger slides along the line to catch over the hook and free it immediately.

THE SLAMO DISGORGER

finger because the reel is smooth on the back edges. And it's got a line clip, which is invaluable for accurate legering. All the spools are filled right up. I change the line about every three months.

At the bottom of the box are various spools of line: some 5 lb (2.5 kg) Maxima for shock leaders; and some 2 lb (1 kg) and 3 lb (1.5 kg) spools for those times when I'm on a lot of fish and can scale up to catch faster. I don't have any preference for the main-line colour, though I like a white or clear line for hooklengths.

I have become very fond of Browning's new high-tech line, which went on sale in 1993. It's called Hi Power. The 0.014, which I've been using a lot, is incredible, because you can't break it. It will be terrific for carp-fishing close in, and it goes down to 0.06. One of the bonuses of being a tackle consultant is that I get the new lines to try out first.

Every pole angler should carry a tub of Vaseline. If you have got a pole float that is sinking a bit too much, you don't have to take a shot off. Just put a dab of Vaseline on the tip of the float – but make sure it doesn't go on the rest of the float.

I'm not really superstitious, but I always carry a lucky horseshoe. I'd just come back from winning the World Championships in Yugoslavia and the little girl who lives at the Lakeland House guest house in Belturbet, where I stay in Southern Ireland, presented me with it, wrapped in silver paper. Her parents live on a farm and have horses. I thought it was just a nice gesture at the time, but that week I won the King of Clubs. How could I not carry it after that?

My rod-bag is about as heavy as my tackle box, and I need the largest holdall available. It has two sections, one for poles and one for rods. This is the top-of-the-range Browning Advance. I've only just got it. I only have one, but I carry five top sections. One is up to 8 m, and I've got four at 5 m. The pole goes up to 13.5 m, but I've got an extension to take it up to 15 m, and another to take to 16.5 m.

I also carry a Browning World Champion pole, which is the one I used to win my first World Championship. The basic pole is 12 m, but all extensions fit it, so I carry it as a spare in case a section of the Advance breaks, which does happen sometimes. I was fishing on Holme Pierrepont in a gale-force wind, and my pole blew off the rest, slammed into a lump of concrete and one section broke. Luckily it broke cleanly in the middle, so I was able to thread one bit of the broken section into the other, pull it through and carry on fishing.

My third pole is the Browning Black Magic, a very light put-in pole I can use for casting overhead. I have some telescopic ones but I don't use them a lot so they live in the wardrobe until I know that I'll need them.

I keep the whips in a separate compartment in the rod-bag. I take several whips with me if I know I'll be using one, but the one I always carry is the Browning Reflex, which is 6 m: telescopic for 4 m and take-apart for the last 2 m.

Despite the weight, I carry an umbrella with me all the time. I never find it impedes my fishing and it keeps bait dry. There's nothing worse than maggots crawling all over you and your tackle when it's raining. And in the winter, that brolly is invaluable for cutting out the chill of the wind. You can't fish properly if you're cold and uncomfortable. Although I take a carryall bag as well, I only use it for bait.

When I'm fishing, I usually wear a thermal, two-piece bib-and-brace made out of a very lightweight but warm material. I use a two-piece so that I can take the jacket off if it's hot. In winter I usually wear tracksuits as undergarments. The most important thing in winter is keeping your feet warm. I use French boots called Chimo, which have a neoprene lining. They are very expensive, but are even warmer than moonboots and easier to walk in.

I have to be selective in the rods I take. As I write, the rod-bag is holding only three because I've been on a run of pole matches: an old Normark feeder rod with a stiff carbon tip; an 11 ft (3.35 m) Browning canal rod; and a 13 ft (3.95 m) Browning Carboxy Match, a beautiful light rod for waggler fishing. Everything is in tubes. Rods and poles are so expensive that it's foolish not to take care of them.

To carry everything, I have a special trolley designed to take the ASI box. It is a combined trolley and stand. I also carry a front footstand. When you are pole fishing, you have to get everything level and comfortable. You should never be straining to balance.

I'm very lucky because I am able to give over a whole room in my house to tackle. It has a workbench covered with pole floats, attachments, bristles, wires and hooks.

Some of my more memorable trophies.

Anyone coming into the room always notices a very large-magnifying glass and light. I use this for all my hook-tying, not only to inspect the knot but also to make sure that the hook itself is not damaged. A spaghetti jar filled with water is also a permanent resident. I use this to balance up all my floats.

Although the quality of tackle has improved immeasurably over the past decade, there are still several jobs you have to do yourself and I keep a drill handy as well. I've made a few adaptations to my ASI box, and things like that.

I don't keep many trophies in my tackle room, just a few of my favourite ones. A superb bronze fish was the individual trophy when we won the World Club Championships in Florence. Next to it I keep a cut-glass vase for the 1991 BBC Essex Sports Achiever of the Year. I was invited to a lunch at their studios in Chelmsford. The tables were full of top cricketers, athletes like Sally Gunnell and so on, all from Essex. I was the most surprised person when they said: '. . . and the winner this year is Bob Nudd!' I had to

give a speech – it wasn't the best speech I've ever given because I had nothing prepared and I was so shocked! I feel very proud of that one when you look at some of the previous winners: Ian MacKenzie, Sally Gunnell and Eamonn Martin.

That was quite a year, because I also attended the BBC Sports Personality of the Year, and appeared on *Wogan*. I was even among the favourites to win the Sports Personality, because *Angling Times* ran a campaign to persuade anglers to vote for me. I don't know how many votes I got, but it was a lot. That said, can you imagine what would have happened if an angler won? Anyway, it was great for the sport because I got a small mention when they ran through the sports, and obviously all the top sportsmen were there. I sat next to a woman who had swum the English Channel both ways non-stop.

As a result of this, and a full-page article in the *Daily Mail*, I got a telephone call from a researcher on the *Wogan* programme. She came down to see me, and spent the day at the house. This happened on a Monday. The next day I got a call saying: "You're on *Wogan* tomorrow night."

They sent a chauffeur-driven Mercedes down to pick up Bernie and me. I went into make-up, where they put some stuff on to stop my bald head shining in the studio lights! It all happened so quickly. I didn't have time to be nervous. I can remember it very clearly. Terry asked lots of daft questions, because he isn't a fisherman. I had no idea what he was going to ask, but it seemed to go well. I was on for about 10 minutes. Afterwards he chatted to Bernie and myself backstage. It was a brilliant evening, and later I got a cheque for £200!

The World Championships, surprisingly, doesn't give out many trophies: gold medals, but not many trophies. That said, I was given a beautiful bone-china pot for winning in Yugoslavia. Bernie has taken charge of that one. She thinks I will probably break it if it's left in my workroom!

Occasionally I am presented with something special, such as a £300 limited edition rod made by Fly of Italy. The trouble is that I can't use it because I'm sponsored by Browning, but it has sentimental value.

SPONSORSHIP

It's easy to give the impression that my life is nothing but fishing, but to get to a stage where I had financial independence has involved a lot of hard work, and ultimately wrecked my first marriage.

In 1986 I finally sold my catering business which by that time had become quite substantial. It might seem a drastic step, but it worked out very well for me. That year I won nearly £13,000. I had split up from my first wife so I didn't need much money to live on. Around the same time I started to get a little more sponsorship money, and I was doing a little work for magazines.

Match winnings are deceptive, however. If you win £13,000, the match has cost you at least half of that with pools, travelling, bait and so on. I declare all my match winnings to the taxman every year because it's not worth try-

ing to hide this sort of thing when you're in the public eye. However, you can only be taxed on winnings from sponsored matches. If you go to a match and everyone is putting in £10, whatever you win is tax paid. In my opinion, if the taxman is going to tax the people that win, those that don't should be eligible for tax relief.

Since 1986, I have won more than £10,000 every season, although I had no idea I could expect such an income from angling when I sold my business. If I had knuckled down to it and spent all my time working, I would be worth a lot of money now, but I wouldn't have had half the pleasure. I wasn't really clear in my mind quite what I was going to do at first, and the idea of being a professional fisherman seemed ridiculous. I didn't even think of it that way. I just knew that I wanted to fish more.

I had some sponsorship from Browning, and my tie-up with Van den Eynde groundbait was just taking off. I had formed a company with Jan van Schendel and Marcel van den Eynde to be importers of his groundbaits. They are so good that I have used them ever since. Even if I wasn't involved with the company, I would still use them.

The tie-up with Van den Eynde was not my first sponsorship. That came in 1984 from a tackle dealer called Stuart Arnold. He was the first person to import bloodworm from the Continent. The quality was far higher than we could buy here, and it's something that has given me a steady business in the Home Counties over the past couple of years. Stuart had a tackle shop in Waltham Cross, Essex. He asked me to fish under the shop name, Arnolds Rods and Tackle, and in exchange gave me free bait, clothing and some tackle. It seems minor league now, but at the time it was a terrific deal.

Stuart and Terry Freeman, who is now director of Browning's UK subsidiary, were the first to import Browning equipment direct from Belgium. Eventually Terry took over the whole business, and asked me to continue the sponsorship deal, but under the Browning name, in 1986. I've been with him ever since, and my backing has increased each year. When I won the World Championships, I got a win bonus as well. My increasing involvement has also meant royalties on products.

In the first year I was paid £1,000. It's now well into five figures. But even more important to me in those early days was that I got all my tackle for nothing. I was listed as a tackle consultant, but it wasn't just a wheeze to get me a few bob. I have always felt that if I take money in sponsorship, I have to give something back for it. As well as taking tackle testing very seriously, I do road shows, tackle forums and so on. I am used by Browning throughout Europe, particularly in France and Italy, though I can't speak either language! It's funny, but I've gone from being English to become more European. I consider that my ties are just as much with France and Italy. I don't think England can ever stand alone like it has done in the past.

Tackle testing is not just a matter of going fishing. You need to think about the product and what it's aiming to do. Sometimes I will ship a pole back at a long length to see how it feels unsupported. I will generally fish with two or three prototypes before the final product comes out. My opinions can be as simple as: 'It wants stiffening in the middle,' or 'We need to lighten the weight but keep the stiffness.' That's where the scientists come in. They will alter the carbon in each section. Poles are never made of exactly the same type of carbon throughout. There are various tonnages, depending on what you want them to do. The highest tonnage of carbon we are using now is 65 tons. Next year, it will probably be even higher. It means that the poles are getting lighter, stronger and stiffer at a greater length all the time. It's a continuous process. As I write, I have only just received the 1993 model, but I'm already working on the 1994 one. As the basic materials improve, a company is able to achieve things that are unachievable at the moment. People think sponsorship just means wearing a flash jacket and having your name put in the paper with the sponsor's name in brackets. But if you are sponsored by a company, you owe it to that company to try and promote its products in every way that you can.

I do quite a lot of charity work. This can range from local club events to presenting the prizes at a Duke of Edinburgh award scheme. I don't do a lot of roadshows — only three or four a year. You have to work really hard at them and it's bound to affect your fishing. The main ones I do now are with Anglers World Holidays. For the past six years, they have been giving me free holidays, and in return I allow them to use my name and pictures in their promotional literature. It allows me to see other countries and to explore their fishing potential.

Of course, you have to do well at fishing, but a large part of my job now involves travelling around the country, promoting tackle at trade shows, talking to customers, retailers, going abroad and putting my name and endorsement on advertising. Sometimes this can take up three or four days a week, but I accept it. It's part of the price for being sponsored, and I'll do it as well as I can.

With Van den Eynde, I've got an extra incentive to promote them because I'm a director of the company. I don't think I could put my name to anything I didn't believe in, but even in the very early days I knew that the product was brilliant. The business here started in a fairly small way, bringing in containers of groundbait and distributing them throughout the country, and in the first year we probably sold 10 tons. It's now more than 100 tons. I had tied up a deal with a national parcel delivery service under which it would deliver anywhere in the country for £2.50 a box. I wish I could get a deal like that now! Continental groundbaits were still very new. Sensas dominated the market then, but we caught them up. We introduced a range of totally different groundbaits used by a top angler like Marcel, and they went down a bomb.

Learning about the groundbaits was a revelation. Amazingly, Marcel keeps the balance of all the ingredients in his head. He won't even disclose to the other directors and me exactly what's in it.

The proof of the pudding . . . Marcel van den Eynde, one of the world's best anglers, proving without a doubt that his groundbaits work.

Groundbaits

These are the Van den Eynde groundbaits and additives that I use most frequently.

Groundbait	Mix with	Main use	Comments
Active feeder	25% brown crumb	Feeder only	Very active groundbait. Feeder empties within seconds as groundbait explodes out.
Lake	Use on its own	Stillwaters	Medium-weight mix. Depending on the amount of water you use, it can be made heavier or lighter. Use it with little water or over-wet to explode on the top.
River	Use on its own	Bloodworm fishing on still or running water	Very good for roach. Lots of binding power and my favourite for bloodworm fishing. I can get lots of joker in very little groundbait.
Surface Cloud	Use on its own	Stillwaters	Good for catching fish up in the water. For squatt, punch and joker fishing. Breaks into an attractive cloud on hitting the water. Because it has very little food in it, you are not filling the fish up. Fish it sloppy or very dry.
Secret	50% River	Hard-flowing waters	Heaviest of the range. The mix I would use if the Bann was flowing hard, or on the big, deep canals in Holland and Belgium.
Supercup	Brown crumb	Canals and most stillwaters	Lightish mix with a very strong aroma. Will take a lot of pinkies and casters.
Natuur	50% River	Flowing water	Contains a lot of hemp. Heavy mix that is good for bloodworm.
Kastaar	Brown crumb	Slow-moving waters	Best for bream, as it's semi-buoyant. I often use this if I'm fishing caster or worm.
World Champion	Use on its own, or mix with Secret or Supercup.	Flowing rivers and big canals	A sticky mix that's good for bloodworm. Will take lots of stuff. Mostly for roach. This was the groundbait used by the Belgians to win the 1983 World Championships.
Hi-pro Specimen	Use on its own	Stillwaters	For carp and tench. Best in the summer when there are a lot of fish about. It contains plenty of particles to attract and hold big fish. Hi-pro will take a lot of casters or maggots.
Canal	Use on its own	Canals or stillwaters	Lighter mix than Lake. Ideal for English canals. Very small particles attract roach and gudgeon especially. Ideal for joker and squatt.
Venkel	Additive	See comments	A roach additive which has a herby, aniseed smell. OK to add it to maggots.
Brasem	Additive	See comments	A bream additive. Beware of overusing it. A quarter-pack will be enough for 7 lb (3.15 kg) of groundbait. Developed by Germany's most successful angler, Wolfgang Kremkus.

Active Feeder and Hi-pro Specimen: two of the groundbaits I've developed specially for big fish.

Angling now provides me with a good living. I earn about £50,000 with all my various projects. This includes small deals here and there, like tungsten olivettes. I had been working with somebody who owned a darts company. He wanted to expand his factory and it coincided with the problems with swans and lead shot. These olivettes have been a real advance because they are better than lead: a tungsten olivette is about two-thirds the size of its lead equivalent.

My income might sound a lot to many anglers, but we have some way to go before anglers can start to demand the same sort of money as snooker players or golfers. The only time we will be able to earn more money is if and when television becomes part of the equation. When that happens, I think it will not be long before we are seeing UK anglers earning well into six figures.

One thing is certain: whoever hits the big money will really earn it. The quality of angling has improved so much over the past five or six years that it's far harder to win now. On a 100-peg match, everyone will have top-quality tackle, 13 m poles and the like, and you are probably fishing against at least 50 people. Fifteen years ago, it was probably no more than 10. If you're going to win and keep winning, you have to devote yourself wholeheartedly to angling. This means not just keeping up with trends, but getting ahead wherever possible.

You have to work harder at finding the matches now. Not so long ago, there were 100-peggers all over the place but they're not common now. I don't really have a local water, although I could say it's Willow Park at Aldershot – and that's a 110-mile drive. A local water is important for your own success. You need a water where you feel really confident about doing well nearly all the time. You can't keep skipping all over the country expecting to win, so you need to build up a network of contacts throughout the country, people whom you can trust to put you on to the right method, tell you how a water is fishing and give you up-to-the-minute advice.

You get this from chatting to people and being honest with them. If you hold back, or give them misleading information, you can only expect them to do the same to you. Local knowledge is so important. You can see this best of all in the National Championships. It's become almost standard practice now for a team to pay a top local angler for his knowledge and advice. I've heard figures of up to £750 being paid.

A top angler will find it much easier if he has someone else to handle all the time-consuming day-to-day details. I have a book-keeper who looks after that side of the business, and I'm lucky because Terry Freeman, Browning's boss, acts like my manager. He set up the deal for this book and for some videos that I did in 1991. He's the perfect manager because I can trust him implicitly, and he doesn't take any money from me for the work he does!

I would love to have a regular travelling companion who fishes on the open circuit but there's nobody living anywhere near me who can devote the same amount of time to fishing that I can. However, team fishing with Van den Eynde Essex Superteam enables me to learn new things. Nobody ever knows everything, or even half of it, in fishing. When you think you've stopped learning, you're on the downhill slope.

I'm lucky in another way because I have a wife who is strong and supportive. That's a rarity for an angler. Fishing is not an attractive sport to most women and I'm very fortunate that my second wife, Bernadette, will come and sit on the bank with me. I met her while I was doing some promotional work for the Northern Ireland Tourist Board and Anglers World Holidays. Every time I went to Ireland, I went to see her. At that stage, I was in Northern Ireland quite a bit, so I saw a lot of her. She would come to England to see me as well, and it wasn't long before we were talking about marriage. We fixed the date long before I knew that I would be fishing in the World Championship team in Yugoslavia.

I had been divorced from Susan in 1984. We're still very friendly and get on well, but it must have been very difficult, being married to a mad-keen angler. I spent a lot of time away fishing, a lot away running my business, and the marriage just drifted apart. Although I'm still close to my daughters, I feel guilty about what the break-up did to them. I suppose I'm lucky that they are so well adjusted. The lesson for any serious angler is that you need a very understanding wife, because it's a very selfish, time-consuming sport.

I'm lucky that Bernadette is so understanding. She was under no illusions about what she was taking on, and what a serious angler's life involves. In my position, her support is absolutely crucial. She has given me security at home, and there's no doubt that her presence has made me a better fisherman. What makes our marriage even better is that she comes out with me all the time during the summer, and at least once a week even during the winter. She even drives home if I'm too tired!

Our wedding was as memorable for me as my World Championship win. It was in Larne, on the coast in Antrim, and it was very much a family affair, though Billy Hughes was best man. We didn't go on honeymoon straight away, though – because the following week was the King of Clubs, and I didn't want to miss that! So Bernie spent our honeymoon on the river bank. We made up for it a couple of weeks later when we spent three weeks in America, visiting Florida and then driving to Mississippi to see my sister Jackie.

FISHING IN IRELAND

Ireland has been kind to me in a way unconnected with fishing. I just wish that I had discovered Bernadette – and Ireland – earlier. I seemed to have an affinity with the country from that very first trip to Ballinasloe. Since then, I've won virtually every major festival except the Benson & Hedges, now called the Ulster Classic. I was lucky enough

to fish that match in the very early days, when there was a huge head of roach in the Erne, and 100 lb (45 kg) catches were commonplace.

Not long after I started fishing the Erne, I heard about the River Bann at Portadown. The fishing here was even more spectacular than the Erne because it was a smaller river and the roach were larger. I started fishing it in the early 1980s, when catches of 80-100 lb (36.2-45 kg) were the norm.

The first time I saw the river was in a three-cornered team match, Essex County v. Barnsley and Trentmen. I had a terrific draw on Hoy's Meadow and weighed in just under 100 lb (45 kg). On the next peg was a young angler called Tommy Pickering, who was already a big name. He caught about 2 lb (900 g) more than me. I fished with a 7 m pole to hand and fed balls of groundbait. Every time I cast

A happy Tommy with the second day catch that made him 1989 World Champion.

A big Shannon bream comes to net. On a big river like this, where the fish are well out, the feeder is usually the only way to catch bream.

in, the float went under. They weren't particularly big roach, not like the 1-pounders (450 g) that were to become a feature of the stretch. My memory of that time is of all the outlandish things we tried in an effort to protect our hands from that big hook. We even squirted superglue all over our hands!

I was very inexperienced at that sort of fishing and I needed much more practice. I didn't really know how to hold a pole properly then. It's easy to fish off your arm at 7 m, but I was trying to fish the same at 10 m, and it was hard work. I hadn't learnt about using the box as a fulcrum. I tried standing up, but it was no better. Now I have learnt the proper way, just using the box to lever the float out, I can fish for 10 hours without any effort.

In those early days on the Bann, the tackle was very crude: 6-8 g floats, 5 lb (2.5 kg) Maxima main line and 4 lb (2 kg) hooklength to size 10 and 12 Model Perfect hooks with no barb and four or five maggots, fished 2 in (5 cm) off bottom. Poles were only 8-9 m, but we moved very quickly to 10 and 11 m. Most of the time we fed balls of groundbait, but I had a lot of success loosefeeding. I even won a big match on the Bann by doing everything wrong – instead of throwing in rock-hard balls of groundbait, I fed soft ones.

It was one of the Easter Bann Festival matches and the river was flowing hard. I had been feeding balls of ground-bait and catching reasonably well, but not fast enough to win. For some reason – don't ask me why – I switched to soft groundbait and started to get a fish every cast. I went from nowhere to winning with 130 lb (59 kg). I suppose that soft groundbait drew those fish up from several pegs away, but you wouldn't normally fish soft groundbait in flowing water!

Nowadays there are not as many roach on the water and you have to fish it much more sensibly. In 1992 I won my section several times by fishing long pole, short line with elastic and an 18 hook. I recently won a Bann match with 59 lb 8 oz (27 kg) of roach up to 1 lb (450 g). Long pole, short line gives you much better control and pre-sentation. I was fishing only 3 g, though I was 15 m out. The other important thing was to use the right-sized hook. I was on an 18. Fishing to hand in the normal Bann style, you would tear out of those fish on a little hook, but with elas-tic they stay on. Many anglers assume that you can't take a big weight on elastic, but I've had more than 100 lb (45 kg) of roach and bream using it.

A weight of 50 lb (22.7 kg) is a good Bann catch these days, though occasionally it will throw up bigger catches. A

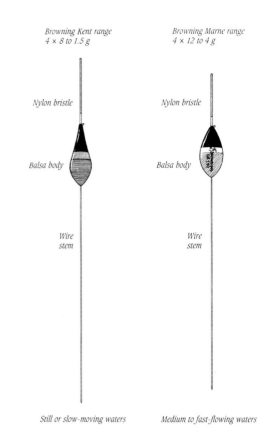

Browning Kent range
4 × 8 to 1.5 g

Browning Marne range
4 × 12 to 4 g

Nylon bristle

Nylon bristle

Balsa body

Balsa body

Wire stem

Wire stem

Still or slow-moving waters

Medium to fast-flowing waters

FLOATS FOR ROACH FISHING ON A LONG POLE

1 lb (450 g) roach is a good Bann fish. There used to be lots around 14 oz (395 g), but the exceptional fish of around 1 lb 8 oz (680 kg) are real rarities now. Another factor has been the arrival of bream. At Hoy's Meadow there never used to be bream, though you could catch them above this stretch. And there are not so many pegs now where pole is the method. It's very often the feeder.

The pole will often produce if there is colour and flow. The Bann often fishes well on the pole around Easter, and again in November. To make things fairer, the best matches mix venues so you fish the lower Bann, upper Bann and the River Blackwater, which is deep and ideal pole water. There's a stretch between two bridges called Verner's Bridge that is packed with fish all through the winter, and you can often get 100 lb (45 kg) there.

For those who haven't caught 100 lb (45 kg) of roach, it sounds an impossible target. But if you gear up your tackle accordingly, develop a steady rhythm and catch roach averaging 8 oz (225 g), you only need to take 20 fish every 30 minutes. And when your float is going under almost as soon as it settles, that's not as hard as it sounds!

The first thing you have to do is adapt your pole tip. In most cases, this means buying an extra tip and cutting it back so that it is stiff. When you are swinging in 8 oz (225 g) roach, they must come to your hand, not round your ankles. A reasonably strong pole is important. I still use a Browning Spiral Titanium, which is seven years old. Another excellent pole for this sort of fishing is the old Daiwa Pro Carbon. I don't use the new ultra-stiff poles for this sort of fishing, because they are likely to break. They're not designed for this sort of rough treatment. The telescopic poles designed for fishing in England for 2 oz (56 g) roach are no good for Irish fishing either. They are just too soft. Look for a good-quality secondhand put-in pole and you'll probably have the right tool.

Floats should be a minimum of 6 g and may be as heavy as 12 g. The heavier you fish, the quicker everything becomes if there are lots of fish around. I usually set up three rigs, but it's limited by the number of poles you have, because this is very specialised fishing.

The old days of size 10 hooks and 5 lb (2.5 kg) line are gone, because the fish have got smarter. You may catch on size 14 and three maggots, but be prepared to fish finer. I would start on a 14, but be ready to go to a 16 or even 18.

The other area of Northern Ireland that has been a happy hunting ground for me is around Enniskillen on the festivals during late April and May. Northampton travel agent Cliff Smart started running competitions after the Benson & Hedges Festival and the fishing was often even better. The fish were running through to spawn and cold weather often delayed their spawning.

The best weight I ever had in a competition was on one of Cliff's matches. I drew Elizabeth Road, a narrow, fast-flowing stretch of the river right in the middle of Enniskillen. I had 180 lb (81.6 kg) of roach there on a 4 m pole from just 5 ft (1.5 m) of water. That day, the fish kept coming and going. During the last hour or so, I had to go across to the other bank with a longer line. Of course, I was sharing those fish with other anglers pegged a few yards away. On my own, I reckon I could have caught 350 lb (158.75 kg) that day. But then, match fishing is about competing against others!

Wherever you fished at the start of the 1980s, there were loads of fish. I was pegged at Trory once and weighed in 104 lb (47.15 kg) to finish only fourth in the

In the 1980s we used to catch 100 lb of Irish roach like this.

section. Pete Clapperton was on the same section and had 111 lb 8 oz 8 dr (50.590 kg). On the way back, he asked another angler how he'd done. He said: 'I've had 111 lb 8 oz 8 dr.' They had tied for the section with a weight like that!

I fell in love with Irish fishing because it suits my personality. I'm a compulsive feeder. I want to throw food to the fish. If I had been brought up on the Northern canals or the Trent, it might have been very different. However, heavy feeding is no longer the way to catch Irish fish. Now it's light feeding and small hooks, even for the bream. There are still some roach – a lot by English standards – but they are not around in anything like the same numbers. I weighed in 77 lb 3 oz (35 kg) of roach in the 1992 Classic, and there was a 132 lb (60 kg) catch, so there are still a few about, but they are not in every section.

Bream play a much greater part in Irish fishing now. They have increased in numbers but not in size, and 3 lb

(1.35 kg) is still a big fish. There are a lot of 1 lb (450 g) skimmers, and plenty of hybrids, which are good to catch because they weigh heavily, and they're less slimy than roach, so they're easier to bring to hand. But they fight very hard and they are very crafty. You will catch them high in the water on very light tackle. You have to fish very light and on the drop for them. If it's 6 ft (1 8 m) deep, I aim to catch hybrids on the drop by having just three or four No. 10s down the line. Perch, especially at Trory, can occasionally produce some big weights – I've seen an 80 lb (36.3 kg) catch – but they don't seem to weigh as heavy as English perch.

In the early days we used large maggot trays to hold 3 gal (13.5 litres) of bait, and often put the lot in. The groundbait now is a much softer mix. I still feed at last 10 lb (4.5 kg) of dry, but use brown crumb mixed with Van den Eynde Lake or River, depending how soft I want it. Mix it up and run it through a riddle. You should be able to squeeze it, throw it, and see it break up as soon as it hits the surface. I put in an orange-sized ball every cast, which works very well on pegs of 8-10 ft (2.45-3m). If the water is running hard or very deep, you need a stiffer mix. I add some white crumb, and perhaps some Van den Eynde Hi-Pro Specimen.

The aim of the lightweight mix is to draw fish from quite a distance away. Irish bream are not always turned on by balls of heavy groundbait any more, but will often swim into a cloud and feed happily. That was my main tactic in 1992, even on the Bann, and I played it very cautiously by fishing long pole, short line with small hooks, and running down the peg. I had to net almost everything, but it brought me a lot of 60 lb (27.2 kg) weights.

The great thing about Irish bream is that they don't fight too hard. If you are using a big enough hook, you can get away with a flick tip and they come out easily. If they will take a 14, I'll use a flick tip; if I've got to use 18s and 20s, I'll use elastic.

Fishing in Ireland, even on the lead, now means a more cautious approach. On double caster I would use an 18, but if I am fishing worm, then I use a 14 or 16. On maggot now it's 16s and 18s: no more size 10s. You have to match your bait to the hook; there's no point in squashing three worms on to a 20. I generally use a 354 Browning. You

don't need a forged hook for Irish bream. I prefer a micro-barb beause I am often using worm and that barb keeps worms on the hook. Often I snick a caster on with a couple of worms.

I hardly ever use a maggot feeder in Ireland. The only exception would be for roach in certain lakes. It is nearly always a medium-sized or large open feeder. You can catch 50-60 lb (22.7-27 ? kg) of bream without putting in a ball of groundbait, especially on waters such as the Erne that are regularly match-fished. The fish have now got wary of groundbait.

Even if you're fishing the pole, it can pay to put a little groundbait slightly further out. I won the final of the Cliff Smart series in 1981 with 103 lb 5 oz (47 kg) of bream from Cornagrade, and though I caught on the pole all day, I had fed about 20 metres out with seven or eight balls. I could almost imagine the fish flitting backwards and forwards between where I'd put this groundbait and my pole line. From then I realized that sometimes fish like an area where they feel safe to feed. I didn't disturb that far line. That was a strange day because I fished long pole, short line and though I caught a lot of fish, it was because I kept chopping and changing all day. One minute I was on double caster, then a small worm and a caster.

These days, I would feed even that swim more cautiously because the fish have grown smarter. The first time I went to Ireland, on the River Suck, I went pleasure fishing and mixed up a huge bowl of groundbait, hurled it all in and started fishing. I sat there for five hours without a bite. Probably two or three days later, it would have been heaving with bream. Nowadays, you will rarely catch well in Irish matches if you put in a large amount of feed. If there are a lot of fish around, I won't hesitate to switch from the feeder to the bomb, which can also mean getting away with a lighter hooklength. That's a good move when fish are shying away from the feeder.

There are still plenty of roach in Irish waters, but with bream now dominating, an angler who wants to win must be able to fish the feeder as well as the pole. In the south of Ireland, rigs are almost the same as in England. The roach are more difficult to catch than in the north, and even the bream are smarter, so you've got to use finer tackle. There are still some pegs in the north where the fish are really having a go, and you can catch 155-175 lb (70-80 kg), but I reckon Pete Burrell's 259 lb (117.5 kg) catch will stand for quite a while.

I have floats made up from 2 g up to 14 g, but they are all basically the same: tungsten olivette and dropper.

I love dace because they're greedy fish and you don't need to fish tiny hooks for them. This gib net came from the Blackwater in Southern Ireland.

Depending on the float size, the dropper might be an AAA two BB, or two No. 1s. If I'm using more than one shot, I try to keep them together. It means less likelihood of tangles. The important thing is that the distance between the hook and the first dropper is less than the distance between the olivette and the dropper.

Bait requirements for Ireland depend very much on where you are fishing, but usually you will need ½ gallon (2.25 litre) of casters a day, perhaps 1 gallon (4.5 litre) if there are a lot of fish. You can buy casters there, but it's better to run off your own so you know they are fresh. That means checking and turning the bait every morning and evening.

If you have an understanding landlady or you're sharing a chalet with anglers who would rather see bait in the fridge than fresh milk, it is not a problem to keep casters fresh. Otherwise I keep them in cold water and change it regularly. You've got to let casters breathe or they will die. Keep them in water for 24 hours, then take them out and let them breathe, and put them back into clean water. They will last for three days like that.

I always have plenty of worms. Irish bream seem to like worm more than anything else. I add worm to my groundbait, cutting it up rather than adding whole worms.

For some matches where I think I'm going to be loose-feeding, I will take 1 gallon (4.5 litre) of maggots, although I have fed as much as 2 gallons (9 litre). Bait prices aren't too bad over there: certainly nothing like as exorbitant as in Denmark or hot countries such as Portugal. It's probably easiest to get most of your maggot in Ireland.

Pre-spawning fish can be ravenous, so you need to give them plenty of feed to keep them interested, or they will move on. You won't always use 20 lb (9 kg) of groundbait, but you need to pack it in your bag. You need to be strong and fit to fish the Irish matches! Sometimes I can't even lift my shoulder bag. To cover me for a week, I usually take a 56 lb (25.4 kg) bag of brown crumb and some Continental mixes of different sorts: heavy and light depending on whether I'm fishing a fast-flowing river or a lake, and buy anything else I need there.

I used to carry two keepnets on every match, but it's rare to catch 100 lb (45 kg) now. However, I always travel there with a spare as it's easy to damage a keepnet.

If you want to keep fish on a pleasure session, it's far less damaging if they are in two nets, though I never put my fish in a net if I'm practising on the venue where I am going to fish; I always put them straight back. Even in Ireland, the fish are affected by being in a net. I always think that maybe

Bream like this one generally like a bit of groundbait – but you may need to switch to a bomb if you find that they are getting finicky.

I will draw that same swim, and I don't want to spoil my chances! Fish seem unaffected and willing to feed the following day if they have been put straight back.

When I'm packing for Ireland, almost all my tackle goes into the car. This means taking everything from large bait riddles to extra bait stands. If I'm sharing with Kevin, running-off bait is easier because he will bring a commercial riddle – a massive wooden box that will run off 20 gallons (90 litre) in under 30 minutes.

Modern ultra-fine carbon and boron rods aren't quite right for Ireland. They have too much give. In the early days we used rods with cut-back tips for fishing Trory because there were so many fish there. You had to fish with a waggler because the fish were too far out for a pole, but you wanted a rod that would winch the fish in, and allow you to swing big ones. The rods we ended up using looked almost like sea rods. Hollow-glass was very good because it was stiff and had little bounce.

Nowadays you still need a reasonably powerful rod. I use an Italian rod called a Match Strong, which will cast 20 g floats but is still ultra-light and has enough flex to be all right for 16 and 18 hooks. It's basically a stepped-up match rod with a slightly thicker tip. It's interesting how a rod has been developed for a specific purpose. I use standard Browning 810 reels, though Kevin uses something that looks like a sea reel. The most important point is that the reel should have a roller bale-arm. With the amount of pressure that you have to put on fish, something without a roller is likely to develop grooves in the bale-arm and the risk of line sticking or breaking.

Reel line is between 3 lb (1.5 kg) and 4 lb (2 kg), mostly sinkers. If I want it to float, I treat it with a silicone spray, and carry another spool that has been immersed in washing-up liquid so a flick of the rod will sink it.

I now use microbarb hooks for Irish fishing. I used to use barbless hooks, but there are not as many fish around now and you can't afford to have a 1 lb (450 g) fish flip off. The other thing is that the quality of hooks has improved so much. Today's microbarbs are so small that they just keep the fish on, but don't impede unhooking at all. I always use a nickel silver hook, which I think is stronger, and either Browning 354s or Tubertini series 2.

To start with, I went to Ireland for a week. Then it became two weeks, three and then four. Now I travel over in mid-April and stay until the end of May, fishing every day. No sightseeing, no wandering round. It's a beautiful country, but all I ever want to do there is fish. The sport may not be like it was in the late 1970s and early 1980s,

but it's still among the best fishing in the world. I can't get enough of it, even after that dreadful World Championships in 1992 when I had a blank on the first day.

Still, that event did bring out one good thing: the Bolognese style of fishing, which originated in Bologna, Italy. Bolognese rods are the ones you see anglers using on holiday, fishing off rocks in Spain, Greece or Italy. When we went on holiday, we used to laugh at them, thinking that the anglers using them knew no better. But for a specific purpose, these rods are unmatched. The slider, waggler and even feeder just can't catch the fish that a Bolognese rod will.

THE BOLOGNESE METHOD

I had seen the Bolognese method several years earlier in Italy. Even then, it impressed me as a method that I could apply to several English, hard-flowing, deep rivers where you need to go some distance to catch fish. The Bristol Avon, the Severn and the Wye immediately come to mind. It's for the sort of places where you may be fishing in 16-17 ft (4.8-5.2 m) of water, and where you can't cast with a 14 ft (4.25 m) rod anyway. You can fish pegs deeper than 20 ft (6.5 m) with it comfortably.

The ideal length for a Bolognese rod is 6-7 m, but they are now available at 8 m, and technology is developing so fast that in three or four years' time I can see 8 m being the norm. Although they are available in shorter lengths, I see no sense in buying anything shorter than 6 m. There are already some excellent match rods at 15 ft (4.5 m), so there is little point in buying a 5 m Bolognese. As I write, Browning is developing a Bolognese rod specially for the UK with a slightly lighter action. They are quite expensive now, but I expect they will become cheaper as more are sold. As long as it's not too heavy and you can cast and fish with it comfortably, buy as long a rod as possible.

The rods are telescopic and the reason they look so odd is that by our standards, they have very few eyes. This is because the eyes actually slide down the pole until they reach a part where they become tight. Near the butt, there is one eye for every section of pole, which might be about 1 m long. They look strange, but remember that you use heavy tackle to pull the line through. You are not trying to cast a 4 × No. 4 stick float. Cheap Bolognese rods are available, but the better ones have a stiffish through-action. Because you are casting a 6-7 g float, the rod shouldn't be too soft.

End tackle is very similar to a pole rig. The float is just like you'd have on pole tackle, but with a thickish balsa tip

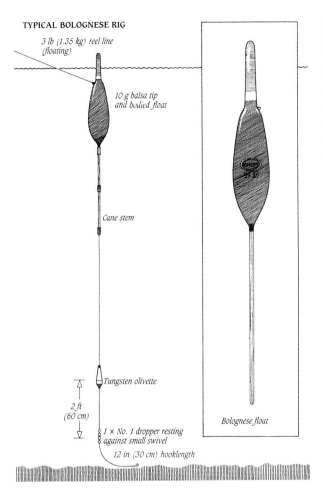

TYPICAL BOLOGNESE RIG

3 lb (1.35 kg) reel line
(floating)

10 g balsa tip
and bodied float

Cane stem

Tungsten olivette

2 ft
(60 cm)

1 × No. 1 dropper resting
against small swivel
12 in (30 cm) hooklength

Bolognese float

equal to a No. 6 shot, because when reeling maggots back fast from 60 or 70 metres. It helps to prevent the bait spinning. Double maggot and especially double caster will spin a lot. A longish hook trace helps to prevent spin, and I tend to wind in a little slower if I am on double maggot. A slightly higher breaking strain, if you can get away with it, makes a difference too. The finer the line, the more spin-ups you get. I know that some anglers hook maggot and caster on alternate ends, so one maggot is hooked in the thick end and one in the thin end, but I have got into the habit of having to hook my maggots exactly the same way every time, and I just can't get out of it!

Don't used pre-stretched line with this rig. You may need a shock leader if you want to cast a long way. With a 10 g float you should be using a minimum of 3 lb (1.35 kg) reel line. If I'm using a shock leader, I put about four or five turns of 5 lb (2.25 kg) line on the reel from normal casting position. It should be connected to the reel line by a full blood knot and trimmed back very small.

Its main advantage over a waggler or slider is its directness. It will hold back against the wind even in shallow waters. On the Ostallato Canal in Italy, it's used in 3-4 ft (1-1.2 m) of water, and there it's fished at 60-70 yd (m). That's an interesting water because it has no flow at all. The Italians encourage the fish to feed by lifting the bait and dropping it back. One factor is that the canal is full of a carp-like fish called carassio which feed very aggressively.

You will not be able to loose-feed with this method. On the Continent, you can use sticky maggots but this very rarely works in England. I've caught roach in Ireland using it, but I've never been really successful with it in England. It would be lovely if you could loosefeed at 80 metres, but it doesn't happen so you have to use groundbait.

The method's advantage is the distance you can fish at. You can't get anything like the same sort of distance on a waggler, and you can't hold back a waggler hard. Bolognese is also a very positive way of fishing because you are in direct contact with the fish. If you are fishing a deep, fast-flowing water, you need a lot of bulk down the line. You can't do this on the waggler. You can fish like this with a big slider, but it still takes time to settle, whereas with a simple overhead cast, just as if you were casting a feeder, the Bolognese is fishing your peg within a few seconds of hitting the water. In 16 ft (4.8 m) of hard-flowing water, your bait gets straight down to the fish and on tight pegging this is very important.

So the method has scope not just on waters that flow hard, but also on slower rivers where pegging is tight, and

rather than a bristle, and cane rather than a wire stem. You want the float to follow the olivette, not the other way round, which is a recipe for tangles. The ideal Bolognese float looks like a big Avon, not dissimilar to the big balsas used on the Wye. It's better than a round float for striking and clearing the water. And you are not going to be hanging on to it too hard. The wind does most of the work of slowing it up. It's made for an upstream wind, but never use it when there's a downstreamer. Because you may be chucking the float 40 metres or more, you want a thick top that you can see at that sort of distance.

The float weight depends on how far you are casting. You can fish Bolognese with 2-3 g if you are not casting very far, but it won't handle 2 BB floats or anything like that. The ideal range is between 3 and 16 g. The set-up is really simple. You don't want strings of shot, just a tungsten olivette and a swivel with a dropper. I use a tiny swivel, perhaps where you want to fish beyond other anglers. The obvious applications are places such as the Severn, and anglers like Dave Harrell have already been experimenting with it there. I can see a lot of anglers doing well on slower-moving waters like the Lower Ouse through Ten Mile Bank and Littleport, as well. Ten Mile Bank can be 25 ft (7.6 m) deep and the Bolognese could be a killer method if the wind is right. Any big, wide river where there is a bit of depth, some flow, and a friendly wind would suit the Bolognese.

I can also see it being used on narrower rivers where the flow always seems to pull a waggler out of position on those far-bank chub swims. With an upstream wind, Bolognese could be devastating. I can envisage using it myself if conditions are right on some of the deep Irish lakes. It's still early days, but as more good anglers explore its potential, we will see new uses and new methods developing. Top match anglers over the next couple of years will all acquire a Bolognese rod and add it to their repertoire. It's just a matter of getting used to taking one with you. Over the next few years, we are going to see a lot of matches won on the Bolognese. It may even play a role in a future World Championship as more anglers realize its potential.

TEAM FISHING

As I write this, the next world match is in Portugal in 1993, with England and Holme Pierrepont to look forward to in 1994. Whether I will be in the team for Portugal is anyone's guess. I didn't make the side in 1987 at Coimbra, and the 1993 match is again on a water that looks very similar, with waggler likely to dominate. There are some terrific waggler anglers, such as Dave Harrell, around and I'm going to have to fight hard to keep my place.

Where possible we try to fish the water at exactly the same time of day as the match, to get similar conditions, but you can't always do this. We couldn't get out to Portugal in 1992, so the team will spend a couple of weeks there as near to the match date as possible. Even acclimatising is important for a match like that. But it also means that we can sort out how we will keep our bait in very hot conditions, find accommodation close to the venue and other things that you can't do by arriving the day before. Of course we are helped by the Steade-fast sponsorship. Accommodation and food for seven anglers for a couple of weeks is very expensive. I feel sorry for some of the other sides in the championships, because they are starting at a disadvantage.

I feel that I'm fishing better now than I ever have done. I've learnt what is needed to fish for England and built up the ability not to panic under pressure. Thinking back to the early 1980s, I didn't have that experience. Even if you're not a nervous person, when you're fishing your first match for England, it can be a very testing time. Confidence or lack of it shows in some people even at club or open match level. They set up 28 rods and think they've covered all their options. But they don't know where to go then. You need confidence in what you are doing, and confidence you are doing it better than everybody else. This can only come from catching fish, winning matches and beating the opposition.

Since that very first match in Switzerland I've acquired more knowledge, and I'm less likely to make mistakes. I know what I'm very good at, which is the long pole in running water. There aren't many people who are brilliant at everything. Even Kevin isn't as good on the waggler as Tommy and Steve.

Thanks to the sponsorship by Steade-fast, England have been able to compete on an equal footing with Italy and France. I think these three sides will dominate this event for the next decade. The Dutch are quite good, but suffer from a lot of in-fighting. Belgium produce some good anglers but they suffer from the same problems. Our biggest asset, I believe, is our manager. I think Dick is worth a point or two on every match.

Dick creates harmony. He's done this by retaining a strong core and not changing the team a lot. I think this continuity has been an important factor in our success, but we've also achieved success from having a brilliant angler at the heart of our side. Kevin Ashurst has the best record in the world, having won the individual title on the Newry Canal in 1982 and finishing second three times. I have known him since about 1980, and I've learnt a lot from him. I've looked to him for guidance on fishing techniques and methods, because he is very shrewd. He's one of those rare anglers who has a brilliant memory. After a while, you are bound to come up against a situation you've been in before, and if you've got a good memory you can recall things much quicker.

Kevin also has what I consider to be a very important factor for success at the highest level – the ability to change methods very quickly. I regard myself more as a mechan-

The Boss. Dick Clegg gave up his personal chance of glory to captain England.

ical angler (perhaps it goes back to my days at Marconi!), but Kevin really can think and change very quickly. Of course his father Benny must have been a great influence on him. He was trained very young, and being a bait breeder he's always had good bait.

For 20 years Kevin has been fishing World Championships so he's been going all over the world, seeing different techniques. In England he was probably on long pole, short line before anybody and he's very strong on all aspects of the pole from travelling abroad and rubbing shoulders with the top Continental anglers.

I've learnt all sorts of things from him, everything from points about bait right down to how to tie a hook. I didn't know how to tie a hook properly until he taught me. The way he showed me is absolutely brilliant. And I'm still learning from him. Indeed, you can learn from anybody. I can learn from one of my club members or a 20-year-old who has just started fishing. You have to be adaptable.

Kevin has the perfect attitude. A lot of very good anglers are nervous when they fish big competitions, but he has absolute control and that comes with being confident that you're better than anybody else when you're fishing. You're certain you're doing it right, and perhaps that has shown itself best in the World Championships, where Kevin has often been without a fish or had hardly anything with little time to go, but he always manages to pull out a few. And he does it time and time again.

I became friends with Steve Gardener through the World Championships. He's an excellent example for any match angler who wants to make the top grade. His main strength is his boldness. He is very quick to change and see what's happening. He's without a doubt one of the top all-round anglers in the country. When he's on fish, he will catch an awful lot and he's very hard to beat. Since he's come into the squad, it's strengthened enormously. He's become a regular member of the team because he's able to fish all methods: waggler, pole and all techniques.

The other regular members of the squad are Tommy Pickering and Denis White. They're very good friends, they're Barnsley anglers and they come from the same clan as Dick, but he's scrupulously fair. He will drop them – and he has – if he feels others will do a better job. Both are terrific waggler anglers. They're very good on the pole too; probably not so much with bloodworm, but they're very good maggot anglers. Tommy is very shrewd, and just seems to flow. He's another natural angler. If you look at Denis fishing, you will see sheer dedication. Even serious back problems don't seem to affect him. I'd put myself

*Phew, it's a scorcher! All
smiles after hearing that
we've won.*

Ian Heaps, master of the pole – big slider. He inspired me to try Irish fishing so I owe him a big debt.

more like Denis, more of a grafter trying to get it all smooth and efficient.

It takes me longer to find out the method. I work at it more like a machine. I don't consider myself anything like the same type of natural fisherman as Kevin or Tommy. But World Championships are ideal for me, because I can work for two weeks and find the method, then put that knowledge to use. My strengths are that I will knuckle down and learn how to fish a water.

You always like to fish to your strength, which in my case is the long pole, but it's not always the right thing to do. I love fishing waggler, but most of the time we don't get much chance. I won two matches on the Thames at Medley in 1991 using a waggler and fishing bread punch.

This stretch flows hard and is fairly shallow. You can't use a pole because you need to fish well out and to the limits of your peg. But on the waggler it was ideal.

We have become a very close-knit squad. We fit together well, trying to discover things, then using Dick as the central source of information. We have a few heated moments, as we don't always agree, but Dick will sort things out, and generally we take his guidance. He has been perhaps the biggest influence on British match fishing, and he's been the most important factor in my personal success. All that I have achieved is down to Dick Clegg.

He is a very good angler, but a very good manager too, because he manages to knit everybody together without too much arguing. If he says something, you do it – even

Kevin does what he says. But he also gives us the freedom to talk. You can actually say what you think without worrying about upsetting him. Our team meetings are always very constructive because we talk, he'll listen and then he'll blend it together and get a balance. He's usually pretty good at guiding us in the right direction. No one can always get it 100 per cent right, but he's never far out.

During the match, he is captain and runner. He conveys information as to what else is happening. We use walkie-talkies to get up-to-the-minute information on what's happening in other sections, but it's Dick who decides if we will change our tactics as a result of what is taking place elsewhere. If you are in trouble he'll be down beside you, trying to coax you through.

As well as having a brilliant tactical brain, Dick is also at the sharp end as far as the equipment is concerned. He runs his own tackle company and this is important too, because in the last 20 years, tackle has progressed faster than in the previous 100, and every year there are new advances. The ability to be on top of techniques and tactics is vital for anyone who wants to be a good team captain. With competition so much more fierce now, you have to keep fishing all the time. You can soon get out of the habit.

I see a lot of teams comprising some very competent anglers, but they will probably never be any more than good because they don't have an organizer at their heart. Behind every successful team is a successful manager or somebody who knits the group together. It's a job that I've never been able to do, even within my own local team. In the Van den Eynde Superteam we have Peter Clapperton. I wouldn't like his job: hours on the phone checking on details, then phoning everybody and stimulating their interest in those matches where 1 lb will be a good weight and you will probably struggle for a bite.

The ideal team manager has to be very shrewd and to understand current methods and tactics. In Dick Clegg, we've got the perfect manager because he is also such a good angler. Administrators are not always good anglers. If he hadn't been the manager, Dick would have been challenging for a place in the squad. But he's sacrificed his own personal glory for the glory of the team.

The ideal manager or captain needs to be someone who isn't afraid of making decisions, even if they are unpopular. You've got to have leadership qualities. In the England setting, it's important to be able to deal with different nations and to be a diplomat as well. I think there are times when every team captain needs those qualities. It's unrealistic to expect a club team to find a manager who

Dick Clegg has to keep a tally of how all the leading teams are doing. He's the only one with the overall picture during a world match.

combines all these qualities; someone who's a good angler but who won't fish. Yet the captain must show that he has no favourites. One of the things that always impressed me about Pete Clapperton and Dennis Salmon has been that they were always willing to drop themselves and run the bank. It shows not only that they don't think anyone has a god-given right to a place in the team; it sets an example to anglers who are not picked. If the captain is willing to do it, then why shouldn't you?

Picking a team is never an easy thing; everyone has got his own view on who should be in it. I am convinced that the best teams are always those picked by one person rather than a committee. By making someone captain you are putting trust in his judgement. He has probably been chosen because he knows everybody's ability. And if he's smart, he will occasionally ask the advice of the more senior members. That shows that he is not dogmatic and that he is willing to take advice. I certainly think that those teams still fishing trials to decide their squads for Nationals, winter leagues and so on are always on a loser. For a start, you shouldn't be competing against one another but fishing for each other. And you have to remember that fishing can be a very unfair sport.

Look at me in 1978 on the Erne. I won the match but there were probably 100 anglers on that match alone who would have done better from that particular peg. If that had been a team trial, I would have got into the team against some much better anglers. I find the system ludicrous whereby the anglers with the top 12 points get into the team. If the best angler draws the worst peg, he's in trouble. If you fish 50 trials, the best anglers would come out at the top; over three matches, there's every chance that they won't.

The more people you can get on the bank in practice, the more knowledge you acquire. What's happening now is that teams like Van den Eynde Superteam, Starlets and Shakespeare are pulling in experts on a particular water or on a particular style of fishing to increase the team's knowledge bank. We have Wayne Swinscoe, who is brilliant on the Trent and flowing waters, and Kim Milsom, who is perhaps the best angler on the Gloucester Canal. In return, they learn about the waters we know well, and specialist styles of fishing such as catching carp. You get a brilliant mix with real team spirit. It doesn't matter that they don't live in Essex.

Practice pays dividends for you and the team. You get a feel of the water, for a start. If you catch well in practice, you will be more confident come match day. If it's been a struggle, you know what to expect and will approach the water more cautiously than those who haven't practised and who may destroy their peg by feeding too heavily.

When we won the Essex division of the winter league in 1992, I did a lot of practice on the Cam. My information about how to fish it with the punch made a lot of difference. Kim Milsom, who was fishing with the punch for the first time on the Cam, came second in a crucial match with 14 lb (6.35 kg). He had total confidence in the method because Tony Fensom, who had practised there and knew the water well, had told him what would work. There are always little things that you discover when practising - depth off the bottom, how the fish are taking it at that particular time, how hard it is flowing – that combine to make the difference of several fish over a match.

However, you can't take everything you learn in practice as gospel. You haven't made too much noise, because there are only six of you. You all catch fish and get a method worked out. Then you turn up on the Sunday, go out on the method and nothing happens. Match fishing and pleasure fishing are two very different animals. The classic example of this is how well you can catch on hemp in practice, but it very rarely works on a match. The only bait I know that actually produces similar things in practice is bloodworm and joker.

The things you discover in practice are whether the fish are willing to feed, the sort of methods that catch them and the way the fish behave. If groundbait puts them right off the feed, it's pretty certain that they won't want groundbait on match day. Come match day, you have to tone everything down, bearing in mind that the fish that are feeding will be shared, not among six anglers but 100 or more. Almost certainly, you will feed less, and aim not at 20 lb (9 kg) but at 6-8 lb (2.7-3.6 kg). I use practice sessions for getting the tackle and techniques right, and to gain a feel for the water.

On Nationals, I think the system whereby teams sign up a good local angler is the direction of the future. Then the local star has to knock everybody into shape, making sure they have the right tackle, that everybody can fish a 12.5 m pole and throw a little ball of groundbait at the same time. While you're fishing, you will learn little wrinkles that may bring you a few bonus fish. Once everybody is proficient in the basic method, a team captain should be trying new methods, chopping and changing, to sort out the best way to feed, the amounts, how far out, even minor tackle adjustments. Even in two or three days, it's amazing how much you can get through if you work together.

The way that the England team works is a good lesson for any team. There are six, perhaps seven anglers competing for a place in the side, but all information is shared. We sit in a line, but if somebody next to you is catching, he will tell you how he's doing it. Dick weighs all catches at the end of each session, but he doesn't just look at weights. He looks at how somebody has handled the situation, how many bites he has missed and things like that. A good angler can look at another angler and see he's doing right, making the correct decision for the situation, even if he 's not catching fish.

For any team fishing, I think a plan is very important; I find it vital for guidance. A good manager or captain can take seemingly unrelated pieces of information and put them together into a strategy. And it gives you far more confidence if you are clear in your mind about how things are going to go. Of course they don't always go that way, so there needs to be a fallback. And sometimes anglers think they know better, and ignore the team plan. That's all right if the angler next to you is catching 4 lb (1.8 kg) bream, but to go your own way will usually be disastrous. It can be very depressing if you seem to be on a run of bad

draws when you fish only individual matches. But when you're part of a team, your performance on a bad peg is going to be more important than the angler who's on a good peg. Most team matches are won on the bad pegs, not on the good ones.

And that's the pleasure of team fishing. If it was an individual match and you drew and thought, 'Oh, I've got no chance,' you probably wouldn't try very hard, or you might even not bother to fish. But on a team match, you are fishing for your section and even one point can make a difference to whether your team wins or loses.

Financially, team fishing is never rewarding. You have no chance of getting any return on it. If you win a competition worth £3,000, you end up with a cheque for £100 by the time it's split between 18 members of the squad and the fees for accommodation, bait and practice sessions are taken out. If you won £3,000 individually, that would be a very tasty pick-up. Team fishing is done for the companionship, the pleasure and friendship you get from fishing with other anglers and the knowledge that you share. A good team who all work together can beat a team of stars who are all fishing as individuals.

The big man nets another. Kevin always seems to winkle out a few, even from the worst pegs.

6

LOOKING AHEAD

When I look through my gear, I have confidence that I'm fishing with the best that money can buy. Regular practice sessions enable me to evaluate new items as they come on the market, and discard them or add them to my already-overloaded box. If I feel a new make of line or hook will make it possible for me to catch more fish, then I will use it. I reckon the tackle I'm using can't be bettered – but I would love a crystal ball to gaze into the future, and see just what will happen to fishing 10 years from now. I'm certain there will be advances that even the most far-seeing angler couldn't even dream of. Setting yourself up as a fortune-teller is a risky business, but here are some of my guesses at where we may be going.

Looking out over the still
waters of an Irish lough.

*Lough Derg the home of
hard-fighting Irish bream*

There are going to be improvements in tackle over the next decade, though in some areas, it's hard to predict what they could be. The director of the US Patent Office said in 1899: 'Everything that can be invented has been invented.' I expect that in 20 years, I'll look back on my predictions and wonder how I could have been so far out!

I can't see much significant improvement in rods. Better carbons and carbon wraps will result in slimmer rods and thinner tips, but the rods are so good now that I think the margin of increased efficiency will be very small. Poles are a bit different because we are looking at a greater length to give the same efficiency. For the next couple of years at least, you will probably get a pole that increases the boundaries by a metre, perhaps more. Not so long ago, we saw 11 m as the standard length. It went up to 12.5 m. In two or three years, I think 17 m will be the norm and you might be adding a couple of extra sections to get 19 or even 20 m. Inevitably, it will hit a cut-off point until a new material comes along, and that material might not yet have been developed.

High-tech lines are getting better and better. Some of the pre-stretched lines from Japan are exceptionally good. What the line-makers are working on now is a pre-stretched line that performs very much the same as an ordinary stretch line. In other words, it's two-thirds the diameter, has just a little stretch and offers the hard-wearing qualities of a normal stretch line.

Reels have changed little over the past decade. They may get lighter, but they are now so efficient that I can't see a new design supplanting what we already have.

Hooks have made huge improvements in the past six years. I never have to change a hook now because a point has gone. You can now buy some that are advertised as 110 per cent carbon (though I'm not sure quite how you get something that's more than 100 per cent). These have a very high carbon content. They are very strong, won't bend at all, but they can suddenly break, because a high carbon content can make the hook brittle. Over the next few years, hook-makers will solve this problem by producing a hook that will bend a little but won't break.

A lot of people were sceptical about the claims made for Continental groundbaits when they first came out, but they've proved themselves, and got better and better. My company is associated with Marcel van den Eynde, one of the greatest anglers ever. He was a pioneer of these mixes with several ingredients in them to do more than just feed fish, and he is still introducing new ranges. It's come a long way from brown or white bread crumb, and I don't think it's unrealistic to expect ingredients to be added that will stimulate specific species into feeding. A Louisiana professor claims he can already do this with catfish. How long will it be before the same thing happens with roach and carp?

This is one area where the French, Belgians and Italians can teach us a great deal. The English have very little understanding of a particular mix and what it is doing. Our groundbait comes ready packaged, but the top Continentals mix their own. They know what to use for big canals when giant barges are coming through to prevent the feed moving and they know what to feed when it's dead still.

I have done a bit of work on this, particularly with one of Holland's top anglers, Jan van Schendel, but I still don't mix my own groundbaits. I've been through the stage of taking pigeon droppings, pouring boiling water over them and sieving them through. Now I buy it in a bag! But if a group of British anglers worked hard on groundbaits and their contents, I am sure that I would have to do the same to keep up.

I think the biggest developments in angling over the next decade or so will be in the fisheries themselves. River fishing is nothing like as good as it was, but the quality of still-waters has improved tremendously. We are sure to see more and more specialist fisheries such as Willow Park, heavily stocked with enthusiastic feeders like carp.

Managed fisheries that are deliberately overstocked are the future of fishing in this country, like it or not. I like fishing matches on these waters because they are so well stocked you always get bites from something, particularly in summer when you see fish topping everywhere in your peg. Your float keeps going under and you are catching fish all day. That's what any angler wants.

In the next five years, I hope to maintain my place in the England team, particularly where pole comes into it. I feel that I am fishing better than I ever have done, and that my knowledge is still increasing. You never stop learning.

I have very few ambitions. I would love to win a National, I would like to keep my place in the England team and now I've had a taste of it, I wouldn't mind winning the individual title again! I would also love to have a year or so in America, where there is some very big prize money and where English tackle and tactics would produce some amazing results. Peter Clapperton has plans to look seriously at this market over the next few years, and he's asked me to join him. Match fishing will become a very different sport if the Americans get really interested. Perhaps then we shall see a match where the top prize is £1 million. I just hope I can get a ticket!

INDEX

A big-bodied waggler is often vital for casting the distance on big Irish loughs.